MY ANCESTOR WAS IN THE

BRITISH ARMY

How can I find out more about him?

by

Michael J Watts MA, PhD, CEng

and

Christopher T Watts BSc, PhD, FSG

D0730624

1992

DEDICATION

This booklet is dedicated by the authors to the memory of

John WATTS   1773 to 3 Nov 1846
Private in the 6th Foot (Royal Warwickshire Regiment)

Percival John WATTS   1896 to 5 Nov 1915
Private in the Royal West Kent Regiment

Thomas Banks WATTS   5 Apr 1896 to 16 Oct 1966
Private in the Northumberland Fusiliers

John Henry HEYMAN   29 Jun 1894 to 18 Jul 1917
Lieutenant in the Army Service Corps

Phyllis Cater HEYMANN   29 May 1908 to 11 Nov 1990
Major in Queen Alexandra's Royal Army Nursing Corps

Published by the
Society of Genealogists,
14 Charterhouse Buildings,
London EC1A 7BA.

ISBN 0 946789 47 9

Inside front and back covers - omitted in first printing

The cover is a montage of facsimiles of the following documents, which are from Crown-copyright material in the Public Record Office, and are reproduced by permission of the Controller of Her Majesty's Stationery Office.

Front cover:

WO 22/76	Pension Returns, Norwich District - 1 Oct to 31 Dec 1846
WO 25/329	Regimental Description Book for 6th Foot - ca 1804
WO 25/919	Service Returns No 1 for 6th Foot - 24 June 1806
WO 120/23	Chelsea Hospital Regimental Register - 16 Aug 1816

Rear cover:

WO 97/8	Soldiers' Documents, 2nd Life Guards - Corporal of Horse Thomas Playford, 14 May 1834

About the Authors

The authors, Michael and Christopher Watts, are both experienced amateur genealogists, with full-time jobs, respectively, as university lecturer (in engineering) and computer systems analyst. Their interest in genealogy began in 1969 with the discovery of an original marriage certificate for Watts grandparents in 1875. Since then they have extensively researched their family history in local, national and foreign record sources. Within the UK their interests stretch, from London, north to Tyneside and Scotland, west to Devon and Cornwall and east to Norfolk. Overseas, material has been sought in Germany, France, Holland, the USA and Canada.

They have published numerous articles, including several in the Genealogists' Magazine, on Merchant Seamen, Army Ancestry, Company Records and Legal Proceedings. They are perhaps best-known for the booklet "My Ancestor was a Merchant Seaman - How can I find out more about him?", which has been reprinted three times.

Both have conducted night classes for beginners and advanced students, and have spoken on a range of genealogical topics. They are particularly keen to foster an awareness of the importance of modern record preservation, and two of Chris' letters on this theme have appeared in the Times. Chris has had the opportunity to speak on three occasions in the USA and to several societies in Australia.

Michael is perhaps best-known for his regular column in Family Tree Magazine. He also edited the Leigh (Lancs) Parish Register Guide. Chris has served on the Executive Committee of the Society of Genealogists for 12 of the last 13 years, and is a past Chairman of the society. He was recently elected vice-Chairman of the Federation of Family History Societies.

My Ancestor was in the British Army

CONTENTS

INTRODUCTION   1

OFFICERS - PRIOR TO 1914

    Introduction   4
    Army Lists   4
    Returns of Service   5
    Purchase of Commissions   10
    Commander-in-Chief's Memoranda Papers   11
    Half Pay Ledgers and Lists   12
    Widows' Pensions and Pensions to Wounded Officers 14
    Other Record Sources for Officers   15

OTHER RANKS - PRIOR TO 1914

    Introduction   17

    (A) - Finding the Regiment Using "Non-Army Sources"

        Civil Registration   17
        Census Returns   19
        Regimental Registers   21
        Chaplains' Returns   23
        Medals and Names of Battles   24
        Miscellaneous   25

    (B) - Finding the Regiment Using "Army Sources" 26

    (C) - Army Sources

        Soldiers' Documents (Royal Hospital Chelsea) 32
        Muster Books and Pay Lists   37
            1760-1877   41
            1878-1898   42
        Description Books   45
        Hospital Records for Chelsea and Kilmainham 46
        Prize Records   52
        Deserters   53
        Courts Martial   55
        Artillery   58
        Engineers   59
        Other Corps   59
        Militia   62
        Volunteers and Auxiliary Forces   64

OTHER SOURCES - PRIOR TO 1914

    Army Indexes   66
    Waterloo Committee   68
    Army Museums   69
    Medals and the Army Medal Office   70
    Vital Records   72
    Archives and Sources Abroad   76
    London Gazette   79
    Indian Armies   80
    Journal of the Society for Army Historical Research   80
    Miscellany   81

WORLD WAR I RECORDS

    Army Records Centre   82
    Commonwealth War Graves Commission   83
    Index to War Deaths at St Catherine's House   84
    Soldiers who died in the Great War   85
    Imperial War Museum   85
    Other Sources for World War I   85

REFERENCES AND BIBLIOGRAPHY   88

APPENDIX 1 - British Army Campaigns and Medals - 1660-1902   98

APPENDIX 2 - List of Regiments and their Records   100

INDEX   121

ACKNOWLEDGEMENTS

The authors wish to express their gratitude to all the custodians of the records described in this booklet, in particular the Public Record Office, for the assistance they have rendered over the years; and also to the Army Records Centre, the Army Medal Office, and the Commonwealth War Graves Commission. They also wish to thank the following individuals for drawing their attention to particular records or providing information about them: Louise Baird, Jim Beckett, Duncan Chalmers (PRO), W D Cribbs (MoD), Jim Duncan, Nell Fletcher, Mike Grimshaw (GRO), H J C Holyer, Sheila Powell, Mrs Helen Pugh (British Red Cross), Derek Saunders, R H (Bob) Smith (GRO) and Frank Turner. The artwork for the cover was devised by Paul Blake. Whilst the authors acknowledge assistance given, any errors are theirs alone. They would be grateful to hear of any omissions or errors, and about any other useful records not included here.

Transcripts of Crown copyright records in the Public Record Office appear by permission of the Controller of HM Stationery Office. Transcripts of World War I cemetery records appear by permission of the Commonwealth War Graves Commission.

My Ancestor was in the British Army

INTRODUCTION

A standing army in England and Wales may be said to date from the Restoration of the Monarchy in 1660 with the appointment of a secretary-at-war. There was no regular army in England prior to the outbreak of the Civil War in 1642; individual regiments were raised to meet a specific local or national need, and were usually named after the person who raised them. Until 1707, with the union of the crowns of England and Scotland, Scotland had its own army - see Hamilton-Edwards[1] - which is not covered here. From 1660 to 1918 (the covering dates of this booklet), therefore, many of our ancestors were drawn into a centrally organized body, which may be said to be a British Army from 1707 and which has left us many records of its activities.

There have been few periods in history, from the middle ages to the 20th century, when England has not been in conflict either with its neighbours in Europe or overseas in defending trade routes or Empire. The continuing need for men to serve in the army must surely mean that there are few families which have not, at some time, had one of their number serving in it.

Reasons for joining the army were varied. For officers, there was clearly the attraction of an honourable and prestigious career in the service of one's country. They were traditionally drawn from the younger sons of the landed gentry. For other ranks, the rewards were possibly more alluring in anticipation, and the glory more satisfying in retrospect, than the actuality of a common soldier's existence. Our humble ancestor may first have "gone for a soldier" as a result of the recruiting sergeant's patter, and promise of bounty, regular meals etc; few would resist taking the King's shilling after several free pints of beer, while many "volunteers" were blatantly kidnapped. At times there was a lack of other employment, and in national emergencies there was conscription. Once in the army, the common soldier faced the notorious rigours of that service - drill, harsh discipline, low wages after official stoppages, floggings, even execution. However, when required, like Roy Palmer's "rambling soldier",[2]

> He'd march, fight, left, right,
> Front rank, centre rank,
> Storm the trenches, court the wenches.
> Love the rattle of a battle,
> Die with glory, live in story.
> He always said a soldier's life, if taken smooth or rough,
> Is a very merry, hey down derry sort of life enough!

The conditions experienced by our soldier ancestor are evocatively echoed by his contemporaries in many writings, of which there is an excellent selection, with an extensive bibliography, in Palmer's "The rambling soldier",[2] and also in Neuburg's "Gone for a soldier".[3]

My Ancestor was in the British Army

For the purposes of this booklet the very general term "British Army" may be defined to include the following broad categories, consisting of units which existed in some form prior to 1914:

Cavalry : Household Cavalry (Life Guards and Royal Horse Guards); Dragoon Guards; Dragoons, Hussars and Lancers,

Artillery : Royal Horse Artillery; Royal Regiment of Artillery,

Foot Guards : Grenadier, Coldstream, Scots, Irish, Welsh,

Infantry : 1st to 109th Foot, Rifle Brigade,

Corps : Engineers, Signals, Chaplains, Service, Medical, Ordnance, Police, Pay, Veterinary, Sandhurst Band, Small Arms School, Provost Staff, Education, Gymnastic, Queen Alexandra's Royal Army Nursing Corps,

Indian : East India Company's forces, Indian Army,

Militia : usually by county,

Others : Volunteers - Rifle (Infantry), Yeomanry (Cavalry); Fencibles.

Clearly there are many types of unit in which an army ancestor may have served and, if one has no initial clues to his service, the choice of places to search is extensive. The majority of soldiers must however have been in either the cavalry or infantry, although the artillery and the Indian forces included large numbers over the years. It is beyond the scope of this booklet to detail all the units of the British Army together with the changes in title and regimental amalgamations. The reader is referred to Brereton's "Guide to the regiments and corps of the British army"[4] for fuller information. A companion volume by Brereton[5] provides a useful "social history" of the British soldier.

The family historian's approach to army records depends completely on whether one is searching for an officer or a soldier (other rank). Regimental historians and genealogists[1] have naturally tended to concentrate on officers, whose personal records are much more readily accessible. However, there were at least eight times as many privates and corporals as sergeants and officers in the army of 1801 - Fortescue[6] quoted the strength of the Regular Army as 23,000 Cavalry, 9,000 Foot Guards and 118,000 Infantry, and recommended adding 1/8 th again for sergeants and officers. For the 1914-1918 War, there are 80 volumes of war dead[3 5] (other ranks) and a

further single volume for officers.[36] These approximate proportions
indicate that most family historians will be interested in the
records of other ranks and hence this booklet will tend to
concentrate on them. In doing so, one must be aware that most army
records are arranged by regiment; if this is known already, one can
gain ready access to the available material. If the regiment is not
known in advance, then there are many possible ways (not all
successful in every case) which can lead one to the name or number
of the regiment; in the following we give careful attention to this
step, often the most difficult for many researchers.

Fortunately there are very extensive records available for
officers and soldiers, primarily in the War Office (WO) group at the
Public Record Office (PRO) at Kew.[76] Most records for the
period preceding 1914 have been deposited there, but it remains
uncertain whether, when and to what extent personnel records for
those who served in the Great War, that is World War I, may become
available at the PRO. Thus it is ironically true that one may trace
every day in the career of one's great-great-grandfather in the
Napoleonic Wars, while failing to locate any official reference to
the service of one's father between 1914 and 1918. (The personnel
records currently held by the Army Records Centre at Hayes are in the
process of being microfilmed by the LDS and will become available
through the Mormon library system - and presumably also at the PRO -
when the records are 75 years old.)

Our own soldier ancestor did not actually record his personal
reminiscences, but he did leave a clear trail in the many army
records which were compiled during his service. Of course, they were
not originally assembled for his (or our) benefit - Muster Books and
Pay Lists were a check on his attendance and pay, while Description
Books were kept in case he deserted. Luckily there are many types of
surviving document which can give us a broad outline of a soldier's
existence and these can be linked with military and regimental
histories to provide as vivid an account of the life of a "working
man" as it is possible to find.

This booklet is divided into three main sections, namely Officers
(prior to 1914), Other Ranks (prior to 1914) and World War I
(1914-1918). The reason for this is twofold. Firstly, the arrangement
of records pre- and post-1914 is quite different, and thus different
research techniques are needed. Secondly, the records of officers are
substantially different from those of other ranks, the former being
much more accessible, especially with limited initial information.

Finally, the authors would like to emphasise to the general
reader that they possess neither military nor historical expertise.
This brief guide is aimed at genealogists and family historians who
seek a way into the maze of records available for an army ancestor.

OFFICERS — PRIOR TO 1914

Introduction

The tracing of officers in army records is a relatively straight-forward process since there is a variety of sources, both printed and manuscript, which can readily be accessed even though one has relatively little starting information. The key ones, which will be discussed here in detail are Army Lists, both printed and manuscript, Returns of Service, Commander-in-Chief's Memoranda Papers, Half Pay Ledgers and Lists and various records relating to Pensions. This sequence is probably the one which most researchers would follow in practice.

ARMY LISTS

Army Lists, which cover the period 1702 to the present day, are the starting point for tracing the service of officers, and it is relatively simple to find their regiment from this source. Many are printed, but volumes dating from the early part of the 18th century may be difficult to locate. Officers who gained commissions before 1727 may be found in Charles Dalton's books[7] [8] [9]; whilst official Army Lists started in 1740, regular annual lists were not commenced until 1754[10]. Those starting their research in London may use the reference sets of Army Lists at the PRO (Kew); others can locate them in large reference libraries for the period required - there is no need to check every year as information is merely repeated.

The table below summarizes the lists which are available; the PRO (Kew) references are given for material on record there - as mentioned above, large libraries have good holdings of all sets of lists except for WO 64 and WO 211.

Army Lists "on record" at the PRO (Kew)

WO 64	Manuscript Army Lists	1702 - 1823
WO 65	Printed Annual Army Lists	1754 - 1879
WO 66	Printed Quarterly Army Lists	1879 - 1900
WO 211	H G Hart Papers	1838 - 1875

Army Lists (printed), available in incomplete sets in reference libraries, also in the Reference Room at the PRO (Kew)

Annual Army Lists	1754 - 1879
Quarterly Army Lists	1879 - 1922
Monthly Army Lists	1798 - 1940
Half Yearly Army List	1923 - 1950
Quarterly Army Lists	1940 - 1950
The Army List	1951 - date
Hart's New Army List	1839 - 1915

The extent of information provided in such a wide variety of Army

Lists is itself varied; so also is the arrangement. For instance, the printed Annual Army Lists are arranged by regiment and an index is included from 1766 onwards; the "record" set at the PRO (Kew) have manuscript corrections. The Monthly Army Lists are also arranged by regiment, but include the location of a unit and the price of commissions; however, they are only indexed from 1867. The earlier series of Quarterly Army Lists included a gradation list of officers in order of seniority, dates of birth and promotions; from 1881, details of service were also given. This continued the pioneering work of Lt Gen H G Hart (1808-1878), whose New Army List[11] contained services of officers, information not provided in the official list. Fuller details of precise information available is given by Hamilton-Edwards[1] and the PRO booklet on Army Records.[76]

It is worth noting the existence of published lists, for medical officers[12], from 1660 to 1960, for artillery officers[13][14], from 1716 to 1914, and for engineers, from 1660 to 1898.[15]

For most researchers, it is sufficient to consult a sample selection of Army Lists, say at five yearly intervals, until the main outline of an officer's service is established. The results of such a search are given below for Emanuel Burton who, according to a title deed of 1818 for property in Kendal, Westmorland, was an ensign in the "King's Fourty Fourth Regiment of Foot". Army Lists in the period 1819 to 1867 gave the following information:

1819	Ensign	44th Regt of Foot	Appointed	17 Aug 1815
		(East Essex)	Placed on Half Pay	25 Mar 1816
1826	Ensign	50th Regt of Foot	Rank in Army	17 Aug 1815
		(West Kent)	Rank in Regt	7 Apr 1825
1828	Ensign	50th Regt	Rank in Army	17 Aug 1815
			Placed on Half Pay	14 Sep 1826
1840	Details as for 1828			
1850	Details as for 1828			
1860	Details as for 1828, but marked as "Unattached"			
1865	Details as for 1860			
1866 and 1867 - not in Army Lists				

RETURNS OF SERVICE

The War Office first compiled returns of officers' service in the early 19th century, based evidently on information supplied by the officers themselves. Prior to then, regimental record offices had kept some details of officers' service, now transferred and available in WO 76.

These returns of service, listed below, may be used following a check in the Army Lists, or they may be referred to directly if one has easy access to the PRO (Kew). (Additionally, the reference room at the PRO (Kew) contains a steadily increasing series of card indexes of names of officers; many of the returns of service listed below in WO 25 and WO 76 are covered.)

My Ancestor was in the British Army

WO 25 /	744- 748	Returns of Officers' Services	1809-1810
WO 25 /	749- 779	Services of Officers (retired) on Full and Half Pay	1828
WO 25 /	780- 805	Services of Officers on Full Pay	1829
WO 25 /	808- 823	Services of Retired Officers	1847
WO 25 /	824- 870	Officers' Services	1870-1872
WO 25 /	3913-3919	Records of Service of Engineer Officers	1796-1922
WO 54 /	248- 259	Returns of Engineer Officers	1786-1850
WO 54 /	684	Records of Service of Artillery Officers	1727-1751
WO 76 /	1- 551	Records of Officers' Services (originally in regimental record offices) (incl records for Artillery Officers	1764-1954 1777-1870)

The content of the War Office returns of service is again varied. The first (1809-1810) merely gives service details. The second and third series (1828 and 1829) also include information about the officers' families, with dates of marriage and children's births; their place of baptism may well be given, as may date and place of birth of the officer, in the full pay return of 1829. Similar service and family details are given in the fourth (1847) and fifth (1870-1872) series.

A typical entry in the Returns of Officers on Full and Half Pay, October 1828, is that for Ensign Emanuel Burton (WO 25/751):

Emanuel Burton
Age on first appointment to HM Service: 26

Date of Appointment		Full Pay	Half Pay
Aug 17 1815	44th Regt	Ensign Purchase	Ensign Reduction of 2nd Bttn
Apr 7 1825	50th Regt	Ensign Restoration without paying the difference	Ensign By exchange receiving the difference
Sep 14 1826	Unattached		

Desirous of Service?: Not at present.
Service: Full Pay 2 years
  Half Pay 11 years
  Total   13
Served upwards of Three years in the Royal Westmorland Militia previous to purchasing into the 44th Regiment.

Marriage: August 11th 1826 at Drogheda
Children: Margaret Rose born 27th July 1827
Not wounded.
Never held Civil Situation.
Residence last 5 years: In Kendal on half pay, 44th Regt Depot, 50th Regt & in Drogheda since going on half pay of unattached.
Signed: Emanuel Burton.

My Ancestor was in the British Army

The Returns of Service of Retired Officers, 1847 contain similar
information, as this further example relating to Emanuel Burton shows
(WO 25/809):

Name, Rank & Regiment	: Emanuel Burton, Ensign, Unattached
Present Age	: 56
Age on entering the Army	: 23
Dates of the several Commissions in succession, specifying whether Regimental or Brevet	Rank : Regimental Ensign by Purchase Date : August 17th 1815, 44th Regt Rank : Regimental Ensign Date : April 7th 1825, 50th Regt
Date of last retirement on Half-Pay and cause of retirement	: Sept 14th 1826. Own request on account of family considerations
State whether liable to refund the difference before returning to Full Pay in consequence of having received it on retirement to Half-Pay	: Liable, having received the Difference, but perfectly incompetent to refund
If under 60 years of age, state if you consider yourself fit to serve again, or if you are labouring under any disability which you conceive renders you unfit, state the nature of it, and how it originated	: Perfectly active and fit for service, and free from all bodily and mental disability
If under 60 years of age, state whether you have any employment which would interfere with your serving permanently or temporarily on Full Pay	: No Employment I have, in vain, long sought it, either Civil or Military having literally no means except my half-pay
If under 60 years of age, state the number and ages of your family, and how many are capable of maintaining themselves	: Children Three Margaret Rose aged 19 years Emanuel Henry aged 17 years just completed a liberal Education, desirous of Employment but no present Prospect Jane Dorcas aged 8 years

In the Royal Westmorland Militia upwards of 3 years, previous
to Purchasing into the 44th Regiment.
Dated at Wicklow this 21st day of September 1847.

Signature of the Officer: Emanuel Burton

My Ancestor was in the British Army

As mentioned earlier Lt Gen H G Hart's papers, though not official War Office returns, can add supplementary information. They include correspondence from officers, and questionnaires completed in response to Hart's enquiries for details to be included in a biographical dictionary (sadly never completed) of Army Officers. For instance, the career of Lt Colonel William Balfour may be traced in the usual Services of Officers on Full Pay (WO 25/801), or else in Hart's papers, as the following example shows (WO 211/8):

STATEMENT of the Services of Lt Colonel Wm Balfour of the 82nd Regiment of Foot with a Record of such Particulars as may be useful in case of his Death.

Where Born: Edinburgh Date of Birth: 16th July 1784
Age on his first Entrance into the Service: 15 years

Ranks	Regiments Full Pay	Half Pay	Dates	Full Pay	Half Pay
Ensign	40th Regt		Jun 1799	With Purchase	
Lieut.	do		Jul 1799	Without Purchase	
Captain	do		2 Sep 1802	With Purchase	
Major	do		2 Feb 1808	Without Purchase	
Lt Colonel	do		2 Apr 1814		
Major		40th Regt	14 Nov 1814		Placed on half pay in consequence of ill health without receiving the difference
Do	3rd Regt of Foot		Jul 1819	Paying the difference	
Do	40th Foot		Aug 1820	Removed to the 40th Foot	
Lt Colonel	40th Foot		1827		
Appointed to	82nd Foot		1828		
Lt Colonel	do		27 Jun 1833		

Retired from the Service by the Sale of his Commission on the 27th June 1833

Lists, and Dates of any Battles, Sieges and Campaigns, in which the Officer was present; specifying the Regimental or Staff Situation he held on each occasion, and the name of the Officer in the chief command.

Campaign in N Holland in 1799. As Lieutenant. General Sir Ralph Abercromby and Field Marshal the Duke of York, Chiefs in Command.

My Ancestor was in the British Army

```
Helder        27 Aug 1799
St Martins    10 Sep 1799
Onds Carrpel  19 Sep 1799
Bergen         2 Oct 1799
```

Siege of Copenhagen. As Captain. Aide-de-Camp to Major Gen Spencer, General Lord Cathcart Chief in Command.

Battle of the Nivelle, Nive, Orthes, Toulouse. As Major. Duke of Wellington, Chief in Command.

Medal for Commanding 40th Regt at the Battle of the Nivelle, South of France. South of France.

Service Abroad
Period

From	To	Station
Aug 1799	Nov 1799	Holland
Jan 1800	1802	Minorca and Malta
Aug 1807	Nov 1807	Zealand
Sep 1813	Jul 1814	Peninsula and France
Sep 1823	Jun 1827	N S Wales and Van Diemens Land
Jun 1828	Dec 1829	Mauritius
Jan 1830	Mar 1832	do

A true extract from the regimental records X Y M...... Lt Col .....

The above particulars from Hart's Papers are virtually the same as the entry in the Services of Officers on Full Pay (WO 25/801), but the latter includes details of Lt Colonel Balfour's family, as given below (of course it is prudent to check all contemporary records):

If the Officer be Married, specify

When	Where	To whom	The wife living at the date of
1810	Dublin	Miss Charlotte Stanley Clarke	Dead 22nd August 1825 Launceston V D M Land

If the Officer has any legitimate Children, specify

Names	Dates of Birth	Where Baptised
David William	23 Jun 1811	Dublin
Charlotte	31 Aug 1813	[Genava] Barracks, Waterford
John	15 Jul 1815	Belfast
William	18 Oct 1816	do
Charles Anthony	28 Nov 1817	do
Marion	31 Jul 1819	do
George Macintosh	19 Dec 1821	Newcastle, Cty Limerick
Catherine	Jun 1824	Sydney, N S Wales

My Ancestor was in the British Army

Purchase of Commissions

The references in the above examples to purchase of a commission, to half pay and to receiving the difference remind us of the system by which commissions in the army could be obtained, until the abolition of this method in 1871. The origins of the purchase system can be traced to medieval times - see Anthony Bruce[16] for a definitive account. In 1159, Henry II introduced scutage, by which a knight could avoid obligation of military service, by payment of an agreed sum. The king could then use this money to finance mercenaries to fight in his campaigns. Mercenary companies were primarily commercial and aimed at maximisation of profit. Any individual or group with sufficient capital could raise a body of soldiers and offer their services to a client. Appointments to commissions in the company and division of profits were related to initial investment. Hence wealthy men would more easily raise a company and the largest shareholders would become the senior officers. Professional expertise as a soldier was naturally a requirement for success, and hence skilled but less wealthy individuals might still progress.

Each rank, therefore, had a financial value, which could be bought and sold like shares in a commercial venture. Kings later reconciled this mercenary role to national needs. However, antipathy to the purchase system was first recorded in 1641 and continued strongly after 1714, with the Hanoverians. Despite dissatisfaction with the basic system, the authorities found it difficult to end it, as this would have disinvested those in office at the time; the alternative was the introduction of regulations to control the purchase system.

By the time of the Peninsular War, as pointed out by Michael Glover,[25] there was strictly no need to buy a commission. At that time, purchase accounted for only about one in five first commissions; the main reason for purchase was to ensure that one could gain entry to a regiment of one's choice. Thus purchase accounted for about half the first commissions in the cavalry and foot guards.

Prior to 1821, the regulation price for purchase of an ensigncy in the infantry was £400; promotion to the next rank of lieutenant was by seniority, provided that the candidate was adjudged suitable - by examination after 1821 - and was willing to pay the purchase price, in this case £550. Of course, the newly-promoted lieutenant would expect to "sell" his original rank to a successor for £400, so that he would merely have to find the difference of £150. In this way a successful officer could rise to captain, major or lieutenant-colonel in the infantry for (total) sums of £1500, £2600 and £3500 respectively (prior to 1821); considerably higher figures applied in the cavalry or foot guards regiments.

COMMANDER IN CHIEF'S MEMORANDA PAPERS

These papers were concerned with appointments, promotions and resignations of officers; they are preserved at the PRO (Kew) in WO 31, for the years 1793-1870. The original applications have been retained together with any letters of recommendation or covering letters from commanding officers (COs) and agents. They are arranged chronologically, so that the date of appointment, promotion or resignation must first be found from the Army Lists, Returns of Service or the London Gazette. One may discover considerable information about a particular applicant or family.

A brief example relating to Emanuel Burton is contained in the Commander-in-Chief's Memoranda Papers for the 17th August 1815 (WO 31/426):

> Purchased Ensigncy in 44th Regt vice Peacock promoted. Paid £400.

> Recommendation from [illegible] concerning Emanuel Burton's good military conduct in His Majesty's Regt of Royal Westmorland Militia.

> Purchase agreed by General the Earl of Suffolk.

Ensign Burton appears to have been one of many caught up in the euphoria following Waterloo; his service on full pay lasted only eight months until the second Battalion was reduced and he was placed on half pay. Nine years later he managed to obtain a full pay commission again by transferring to another Regiment (WO 31/552):

> April 7th 1825   50th Foot
> Ensign Emanuel Burton from the half-pay 44th Regt.

Even this change of Regiment did not result in much active service and Ensign Burton returned to half pay after a further 1 year and 5 months. As noted above, in the 1847 Returns of Service, this retirement was for family considerations following his marriage in August 1826. The Commander in Chief's Memoranda Papers contain a reference to Ensign Reynolds, who paid £150 to Ensign Burton for the transfer (WO 31/561):

> September 14th 1826   50th Foot
> Ensign Henry Reynolds from the half pay to be Ensign vice
> Emanuel Burton who exchanges receiving the difference.

These papers also include a letter written personally by Emanuel Burton (WO 31/561):

My Ancestor was in the British Army

Drogheda
Sept 5th 1826

Sir,
>   Being desirous to go on Half Pay,
> as soon as it can be accomplished, and
> receiving the difference; may I request the
> favor of your expediting the necessary
> arrangements; and if necessary beg a
> reference to Major Anderson Com-
> manding, now in Belfast.
>   I have the honor to be
>   Sir
>   Your most obedient
>   Humble servant
>   Emanuel Burton
>   Ensign 50th Regt

The Military Secretary

These brief examples show how the Memoranda Papers can expand the outline available from Army Lists or Returns of Service. Extensive family biographies were derived from these papers by Hamilton-Edwards,[1] who quoted other letters, e.g. "memorials and prayers" for advancement or promotion. Glowing references or good connections could be indispensable to progress in the army.

HALF PAY LEDGERS AND LISTS

Until 1871 officers were not entitled to a pension as of right; when they wished to retire, they either sold their commissions or went on to half pay. Responsibility for payment of half pay and pensions rested with the Paymaster-General, amongst whose records are many that may be of use.

PMG	4	Army Establishment Half Pay	1737-1921
PMG	5	Commissariat Half Pay, Pensions, etc	1834-1855
		(from 1840 includes widows' pensions)	
PMG	6	Army Establishment Foreign Half Pay, Pensions, etc	1822-1885
		(for foreign corps)	
PMG	7	Army Establishment, Hanover, Foreign Half Pay	1843-1862
		(mainly to King's German Legion)	
PMG	8	Army Establishment, Hanover, Chelsea Out-Pensions	1844-1877
PMG	9	Army Establishment, Pensions for Wounds	1814-1921
PMG	10	Army Establishment, Compassionate List & Royal Bounty	1812-1916
PMG	11	Army Establishment, Widows' Pensions	1810-1920
PMG	12	Ordnance Half Pay, Pensions etc	1836-1875
PMG	13	Militia, Yeomanry and Volunteers Allowances	1793-1927
PMG	14	Army Establishment, Miscellaneous Books	1720-1861

My Ancestor was in the British Army

As may be seen from the "retirement" of Emanuel Burton in 1826, he managed to obtain the "difference" of £150 from Ensign Reynolds and was also placed on half pay of 3/- per day. He continued to hold a commission so that he was in theory available for future service, indicating that half pay could be regarded either as a retainer or as a pension. It is clear from Emanuel Burton's Return of Service for 1847 (see page 7) that he hoped to be able to return to full pay without refunding the difference; one may therefore conclude that half pay was treated as a legitimate emolument for an officer while not in service, whatever the reason. In this respect he was clearly in a much better position than the average soldier, even though he might not be very well off by the standards of officers and gentlemen of the time.

Much interesting information may be obtained from Half Pay Ledgers and Lists. For Emanuel Burton, they gave his whereabouts from 1829 until his death in 1865; clearly such details can save much unrewarding searching, particularly when the subject decided to emigrate! Some extracts from Half Pay Ledgers concerning Ensign Emanuel Burton are given below. He received 3/- per diem; as he was paid quarterly in arrears, he obtained typically £13 10s.

PMG 4 /	Year	At	Agent
176	1829	Drogheda	Greenwood & Co
205	1838	Dublin	Greenwood & Co
216	1853	17 Capel St Dublin	R.H.Cox
	(to 31 March)		
218	1853	119 Leonard St New York	Cox and Hammersley
	(from 1 April)		
	to 1856	240 Fulton St Brooklyn N.Y.	Cox and Hammersley
		163 Sands St Brooklyn N.Y.	Cox and Hammersley
224	1862	81 Sands St Brooklyn N.Y.	Cox & Co
	to 1865		
	(31 March)		
226	1865	No address, amount or agent entered	
	(1 April to 30 June)		

Emanuel Burton died on the 3rd April 1865 in Brooklyn; his death was not recorded in the half pay ledgers, which are however often annotated with such information.

It is worth noting that the monies were often collected on the officer's behalf by agents, and that some authority was needed for this. Such authorization was recorded in Enrolment Books of letters of attorney and probate (AO 15); a search in the 1826-27 volume revealed the following for Emanuel Burton. (AO 15/151, fo 338)

My Ancestor was in the British Army

27 Jan 1827	A like Letter from Ensign Emanuel Burton upon Half Pay unattached dated the 4th Jany 1827. Empowering Messrs Greenwood, Cox & Hammersley as aforsd jointly and severally.	
Witness	Thomas Henry	E Burton

Further registers and lists of half pay officers are contained in classes WO 23 (Royal Hospital Chelsea, Chelsea Registers, etc), WO 24 (Establishments) and WO 25 (Registers, Various). A selection of material available is given below.

WO 23 /	66 -	78	Registers of Half Pay Officers (arranged alphabetically)	1858-1894
	79 -	81	ditto for Officers of Foreign Regiments	1858-1876
	82		ditto for Artillery and Engineers	1815-1874
WO 24 /	660 -	747	Lists of those entitled to half pay (arranged by regiment)	1713-1809
	748 -	762	ditto for British-American forces	1783-1813
WO 25 /	2979 -	2989	Half pay and retired pay lists	1712-1763
	2990 -	3004	Registers of warrants for half pay and retired pay	1763-1859
	3005 -	3008	Half pay - miscellaneous lists and	1811-1858
	3013 -	3019	registers	

WIDOWS' PENSIONS and PENSIONS TO WOUNDED OFFICERS

There was some provision for the widows and dependents of officers killed on active service. For officers' widows with an income of less than £30 per annum, there were, from 1818, fifteen annuities available under the will of Col John Drouly. Pensions to widows, children or dependent relatives might also be paid out of the Royal Bounty and the Compassionate Fund. A table of some material available at the PRO (Kew) is given below; material for commissariat, foreign and ordnance officers or their widows may be found in other PMG classes (see table on page 12).

PMG 9			Army Establishment, Pensions for Wounds	1814-1921
PMG 10			Army Establishment, Compassionate List	1812-1916
			and Bounty - includes Drouly Annuities for	1870-1882
PMG 11			Army Establishment, Widows' Pensions	1810-1920
			- includes Drouly Annuities for	1827-1870
			and for	1882-1920
WO 23 /	83 -	87	Registers - Pensions for Wounds	1815-1892
WO 23 /	88 -	92	Registers - Widows' Pensions and	1815-1892
WO 23 /	105 -	113	Drouly Annuities	
WO 23 /	114 -	123	Registers - Compassionate List and Bounty	1858-1894

OFFICERS - PRIOR TO 1914

WO	24 /	804- 883	Ledgers - Widows' Pensions and	1713-1829
			Drouly Annuities	
WO	25 /	3020-3045	Pensions to Widows of Full Pay Officers	1735-1811
	/	3046-3057	Pensions to Widows of Half Pay Officers	1755-1778
	/	3069-3107	Registers of Warrants and Application	1807-1856
			Papers for Widows' Pensions and Bounty	
	/	3108-3125	Widows' Pensions - Compassionate Papers,	1748-1851
			Miscellaneous Papers, Registers and Indexes	

It is worth noting that lists of names of those receiving Royal Bounty or Compassionate Allowances, during the period 1812 to 1820, are contained in House of Commons Journals[17]. The 1818 list included reference to many killed at Waterloo; for example, Anne Maria Currie was to receive £150 per annum, from 19th June 1815, being the "widow of Lt Col Edward Currie of the 90th Foot, who was killed at Waterloo; she being left with three children unprovided for". (Other ranks rarely featured in these lists. An exception, in the 1813-14 list, was Alexander Hopkins, "Private Soldier in the 52nd Regt of Foot, for his good conduct at the Battle of Busaco, wherein he took the French General Simon, Prisoner". He received £20 per annum from 13th October 1813.)

Other Record Sources for Officers

Sandhurst is popularly associated with the training of officers. However, the Royal Military Academy there was formed in 1947 by the merger of the Royal Military College (formed in 1800 at Great Marlow but moved to Sandhurst in 1812) and the Royal Military Academy, **Woolwich**, which had been founded in 1741. The latter institution had been formed so that the Royal Engineers and the Royal Artillery could train their officers before they were granted commissions. (There was no purchase system in these corps and promotion was by seniority.) The following classes of records of the cadets who trained at these establishments are held at the Royal Military Academy, Sandhurst.

WO 149 Royal Military Academy, Woolwich, Registers of Cadets 1790-1939
WO 151 Royal Military Academy, Sandhurst, Registers of Cadets 1806-1946

Militia are discussed more fully below on page 62, but the main sources for Militia Officers' records are summarised here.

HO 50	Military Correspondence - including lists	1782-1840
	of commissions in Militia and Volunteers	
HO 51	Military Entry Books - including commissions,	1758-1855
	appointments and warrants relating to Militia,	
	Volunteers, Yeomanry and Ordnance	
WO 68	Militia Records - including Officers' services	1759-1925

My Ancestor was in the British Army

For those commencing their search for officers at the PRO (Kew), it is worth repeating that there is a steadily increasing series of card indexes of names of officers. These card indexes, and their location, are listed in PRO Information Leaflet No 36, Means of Reference at Kew.[84] The cards themselves may include some family details and dates of marriage. They cover material from the following:

WO 25 /	744- 748	Returns of Officers' Services	1809-1810
WO 25 /	749- 779	Services of Officers (retired) on Full and Half Pay	1828
WO 25 /	780- 805	Services of Officers on Full Pay	1829
WO 25 /	808- 823	Services of Retired Officers	1847
WO 25 /	824- 870	Officers' Services	1870-1872
WO 25 /	3090-3107	Application Papers for Widows' Pensions and Bounty	1807-1856
WO 25 /	3913-3919	Records of Service of Engineer Officers	1796-1922
WO 43		Secretary at War: Correspondence: Selected "Very Old Series" and "Old Series" Papers (WO 42, see below, formed from this class)	1809-1857
WO 76		Records of Officers' Services (originally in regimental record offices)	1764-1954
WO 76 /	399- 417	Forester Brigade Group	
WO 76 /	420- 460	Highland Brigade Group	

There are many sources for further information on officers which may be followed up in individual cases. Among these are:

WO 25 /	3239-3245	Reports of Officers' Marriages	1830-1882
WO 32 /	8903-8920	Registered Files: General Series Certificates (as for WO 42, below)	1777-1892
WO 42		Certificates of Births, Baptisms, Marriages, Deaths and Burials	1755-1908
WO 138		Selected Personal Files (closed for 75 years after closure of file)	1830-1963

Records of courts martial for officers and for other ranks are described together on pages 55 to 57.

OTHER RANKS — PRIOR TO 1914

Introduction

The first major objective in the search for an ancestor soldier's career is to discover in which regiment he served. The available documents are mostly arranged by regiment but unfortunately there is no index for soldiers who served in the ranks (unlike officers, for whom there are Army Lists). Here, we concentrate on the problem of finding the regiment, since this is a common hurdle for many researchers.[19] The possibility of discovering the regiment using "non-army sources" is first explored, i.e. by making use of other information available, before visiting the Public Record Office at Kew. If this does not succeed, then one must visit the PRO and search in the various "army sources" which are preserved there - this technique is described next. Finally the sources themselves are covered in detail - we assume of course that the searcher will find the right regiment, possibly after many trials and tribulations. The extensive range of army documents now beckons to the eager genealogist and it is almost certain that these will yield more details for the "common man" than could be found for many other occupations.

(A) - FINDING THE REGIMENT USING "NON-ARMY SOURCES"

There are very many "non-army sources", any of which may lead to the desired information regarding the regiment. None of these sources is guaranteed to lead to success, but all the relevant ones should be tried before turning to the army sources at the PRO (Kew).

Civil Registration

After 1837 (in England and Wales) or 1855 (in Scotland), it is quite possible to find a reference to a soldier's regiment on a birth, marriage or death certificate. For instance, the death certificate for James Sells included the following information:

My Ancestor was in the British Army

When and where died	Name and surname	Age	Occupation	Cause of death
Second June 1843 Britten St Chelsea	James Sells	48 years	Beer Retailer Pensioner of Chelsea Hospital 7th Regiment of Foot	Consumption

In this case it was simple to proceed to the Soldiers' Documents, WO 97 (see page 32). These showed that he had been born at Eastchurch, Kent, had enlisted at Dover aged 18 on 8th December 1815 and had served with the Royal Fusiliers (or City of London Regiment, i.e. the 7th Regiment of Foot) until his discharge, still as a Private, to a pension of 9d a day on 7th May 1826 at Dover (WO 97/292). The searcher was very fortunate here - James Sells was one of those inconsiderate ancestors who died before the 1851 Census, leaving a major problem in finding a birthplace.

The death of our own soldier ancestor, John Watts, left us only this tantalising clue:

When and where died	Name and surname	Age	Occupation	Cause of death
Third of November 1846 at Hasbro	John Watts	73 years	Soldier	Diseased stomach Certified

Marriage certificates may also contain the required information about the regiment. Here are some extracts from an example which gives evidence of two generations of soldiers. It refers to a ceremony at the Parish Church in Liverpool; the address column is omitted below - both parties lived in Clifford Street.

When married	Name and surname	Age	Condition	Rank or profession	Father's name and surname	Rank or profession of father
12th August	James White	Minor	Bachelor	Drummer in H M 46 Regt of Foot	Thomas White	Soldier
1851	Mary Ann Honey	Minor	Spinster		Joseph H Honey	Mariner

OTHER RANKS - PRIOR TO 1914

My Ancestor was in the British Army

Census Returns

It is quite possible to find a reference to an Army career in the Census Returns of 1841, 1851, 1861, 1871, 1881 or 1891. For instance, in the 1861 Census for Ludham in Norfolk, we found the family of Samuel Goodens: (RG 9/1197)

Name and Surname	Relation to Head of Family	Condition	Age	Rank Profession or Occupation	Where Born
Samuel Goodens	Head	Mar	47	Chelsea Pensioner and Agr Labourer	Ludham Norfolk
Joana do	Wife	Mar	47		Cork Ireland
Catherine do	Dau		13		Poona East Indies

It is clear that Samuel must have served at least in Ireland and India, but there is no indication as to his regiment. However, since he had a daughter born abroad, it would be sensible to check in the Indexes to Regimental Registers of Birth at St Catherine's House. (See next section for details of Goodens births found there.)

A further example of some census entries that give a possible indication of a military career was found in the 1851, 1861 and 1871 Census Returns for Happisburgh, Norfolk. In this case, one can also note the variations which can occur in recorded name and birthplace.

Name and Surname	Relation to Head of Family	Age	Rank Profession or Occupation	Where Born
1851 (HO 107/1808)				
Edward Smith	Head	37	Farm Lab	Lessingham Norfolk
Elizabeth Smith	Wife	36		Prescot Nr Liverpool
Henry Hasplink	Son	8		W Indies
1861 (RG 9/1199)				
Edward Smith	Head	47	Pauper	Lessingham Norfolk
Elizabeth Smith	Wife	46		Ireland
Henry Smith	Son	18	Ag Lab	Jamaica
1871 (RG 10/1795)				
Henry Geo Hasplink (and family)	Head	29	Labourer on Farm	Hill New Castle Jamaica India (sic)
Elizth Smith	Mother	56		Prescott

My Ancestor was in the British Army

Following the discovery of such a census entry - involving the birth of children abroad - there are two methods of proceeding. As discussed above, one may go to the Indexes to Regimental Registers of Birth. (This was successful for the Hasplink family and the results are quoted in the next section.) However, it may be that there are no relevant entries for children of that family. In this case, the location referred to in the birthplace column of the census return can be used.

As Henry Hasplink's place of birth would seem to be Jamaica, the Monthly Returns (either WO 17 or WO 73, see page 24) for that Depot may be consulted at the PRO (Kew) to find the Regiments there in 1843; these were the Royal Artillery, the Royal Engineers, 48th, 60th, 77th and 82nd Foot (WO 17/2033). One can then search either the Muster Books (WO 10, 11 or 12) or the Soldiers' Documents (WO 97) for the six units stationed in Jamaica for his father. (He was another Henry Hasplink, serving in the 60th Foot, having enlisted aged 15 at Dublin in the 81st Foot in September 1820 (WO 97/731).)

It is difficult to state what proportion of soldiers or pensioners would have had their regiment quoted in the Census Return. A check on the 1851 Census for Kendal, Westmorland, which had a population of 11,829 revealed 14 pensioners and soldiers, but in only four cases was the regiment given. Extracts from some of these census entries are given below (from HO 107/2442):

Address	Name	Age	Rank Profession or Occupation	Where Born
Peartree Cottages	John Cropper and family	53	Army Pensioner and Sergeant-Major of Yeomanry Cavalry	Lancs Manchester
Highgate	Charles Gaze	29	Sergeant of 55th Regiment	Norfolk Burgh
Fellside Road	William Rigg	75	Chelsea Pensioner & Woollen Handloom Weaver	Westmorland Kendal
Strickland-gate (No 17)	William Carradus	67	Chelsea Pensioner 25th Foot Regt	Lancs Liverpool
Strickland-gate	Patrick Flood	68	Tailor and Chelsea Pensioner	Ireland
Strickland-gate	James M Pennington	65	Late Paymaster in the Army (48th Regt)	East Indies

OTHER RANKS - PRIOR TO 1914

My Ancestor was in the British Army

If one has information about a Barracks where an ancestor soldier was stationed, then clearly the relevant Census Return should be sought. Examples of published census transcripts are those for Maindy Barracks, St John's Parish, Cardiff[20] in 1881 and for Bradford Moor Barracks[21] in 1851.

The whereabouts of every regiment on the census nights of 1851, 1861, 1871, 1881 and 1891 has been compiled by Mr H J C Holyer, 10 Masonsfield, Mannings Heath, Horsham, West Sussex RH13 6JP; enquiries should be accompanied by £1 and SAE/IRCs.

Regimental Registers, Chaplains' Returns

Apart from the familiar registers of births, marriages and deaths kept at St Catherine's House, there are "non-statutory" registers relating to births/baptisms, marriages and deaths/burials of soldiers and their families. The separate series of indexes may well be used as a starting place for a search for a soldier ancestor. These registers clearly originated with the army, but they are now preserved by the Registrar-General, and are quite separate from the main army collections at the PRO (Kew). Currently they are not available in microfilm or microfiche form.

There are broadly speaking two major series of documents for Army personnel available at St Catherine's House:

1. Regimental Registers (1761-1924)

These are registers of births, baptisms, marriages and burials of soldiers or members of their families and were compiled by regiment. The regiments and the covering dates for each one are quoted in "A List of Regiments, Corps and Depots from which Records of Marriages, Births and Baptisms and Deaths have been received"; this list is on the open shelf at St Catherine's House with the associated indexes. A summary of some information from the list has been incorporated in Appendix 2.

All births and baptisms for the period 1761 to 1924 are covered by the nine large black and red volumes of indexes in the public search room at St Catherine's House. (Army Births and Baptisms, AB 91.)

An example of the entries found in the index is given below for the Hasplink family. As mentioned above in the section on "Census Returns", Henry Hasplink had been born in Jamaica about 1843. The index to births and baptisms confirmed this as well as providing data on other members of the family. Most importantly, the regiment of the father is given, so that army records at the PRO (Kew) can now be used.

OTHER RANKS - PRIOR TO 1914

My Ancestor was in the British Army

Surname & Name of Child	Station	Year	Regiment or Register	Vol	Page
Hasplink Chas.W.	Quebec	1835	60th	1076	7
Chas.W.	Quebec	1845	60th	149	148
Harriett	Templemore	1833	60th	1077	24
Harriett	Corfu	-	Ion.Is.	2	50
Harriett	Corfu	-	Ion.Is.	11	122
Henry G.	Jamaica	1842	60th	1076	3
John H.	Corfu	-	Ion.Is.	2	45

A second example relates to the Goodens family, also mentioned above under "Census Returns". Again the required regimental information is given. A full certificate of birth/baptism may be ordered in the usual way from St Catherine's House.

Surname & Name of Child	Station	Year	Regiment or Register	Vol	Page
Goodens Sarah	Dublin	1840	22nd Foot	915	54
Samuel	Poona	1843	do	915	61
Mary E	Poona	1844	do	915	64
Joseph	Coloba	1845	do	915	69
John	Coloba	1845	do	915	69
Catherine	Poona	1847	do	915	74

As in the previous example, one can now go directly to the Soldiers' Documents (WO 97) to find the dates of Samuel Goodens' enlistment and discharge, before proceeding to Muster Books and other documents.

Marriages and burials in the Regimental Registers have only been partially indexed and this card index is not directly accessible to the public; however, requests for a search in it are dealt with in a friendly manner by staff at the General Register Office (St Catherine's House). Application may either be made by post or in person. Approximately half the available material has been indexed, starting with the cavalry, foot guards and the earlier foot regiments; if one knows of a specific regiment (from the birth indexes or other searches), it would be sensible to ask for a search to be made for a missing marriage or burial in the relevant (and possibly unindexed) volume of the regimental registers.

An example of an entry in a marriage register was obtained by enquiring whether Henry Hasplink's parents had been married within the auspices of the 60th Regiment. A search in the unindexed registers showed that Private Henry Hasplink, a bachelor, had married Elizabeth Wilson, spinster, at St Pauls, Dublin on 16th June 1832. (Volume 1076 of Regimental Registers).

2. Chaplains' Returns (1796-1880)

In 1796 the Army Chaplains' Department was officially formed under a Chaplain-General and their records of baptisms, marriages and burials at stations abroad commence also in that year. A separate series of indexes relating to these registers is therefore available at St Catherine's House. Slim printed volumes cover the whole period from 1796 to 1880 for each of the three major events: births, marriages and deaths. For example:

Index	Surname & Name of Child	Station	Year	Reference (page no)
Birth	Watts Elizabeth	Gibraltar	1840-3	91
Marriage	Watts John	Trinidad	1834	515
Death	Watts Jane	Madeira	1814	270

This series of Returns is continued by further volumes whose indexes are also available on the search room shelves. These include the following:

Index to	Covering Dates	Comments
Army Returns - Births (serving out of UK)	1881 - 1905 1906 - 1955	Printed volumes Typescript volumes
Army Returns - Marriages (from regiments)	1881 - 1905 1906 - 1965	Printed volumes Typescript volumes
Army Returns - Deaths (serving out of UK)	1881 - 1905 1906 - 1950	Printed volume Typescript volumes - from 1886 includes age of deceased
War Deaths: Natal & African Field Forces	1899 - 1902	Two separate volumes
Army Officers	1914 - 1921	One volume
Army Other Ranks	1914 - 1921	Thirteen volumes
Army Officers	1939 - 1945	One volume
Army Other Ranks	1939 - 1948	Four volumes

My Ancestor was in the British Army

Medals and Names of Battles

Many people start their search for an army ancestor with some family tradition such as: "Your grandfather received a medal for his services at Kandahar in 1880", but the medal is now lost. "One of our ancestors fought in a Norfolk regiment at Waterloo" was the vague clue which started the authors on their delving into army documents[19] and thence to the writing of this booklet. Similarly, oral tradition may recall service at some particular place overseas.

Where references to medals are concerned, there are printed lists of some of the more famous awards e.g. the VC, DSO, DCM, the Army of India Medal 1799-1826, the Military General Service Medal 1793-1814. (See references 47 to 51). However, for most medals one would have to visit the PRO (Kew) to consult the various Medal Rolls (WO 100 to WO 102; see pages 70-71 below). These medal rolls are available on microfilm at Kew and also at other libraries e.g. Mormon Family History Centres.

If one wishes to identify a regiment from some family tradition about a medal, one may start by consulting Norman's "Battle Honours of the British Army",[44] which has a comprehensive index. To continue with the example of Kandahar, the chapter on the Second Afghan War shows that the honour for the battle of Kandahar on the 1st September 1880 is borne by no less than 27 units, including the 9th Lancers, Foot Regiments Nos. 7, 60, 66, 72, 92 and numerous forces of the Indian Army. The search for the regiment has been narrowed quite a lot; the next step would involve a search in army records at Kew, either in the Medal Rolls (WO 100 to WO 102) or in the Muster Books and Pay Lists (WO 12 etc.) for these particular regiments.

A similar situation prevails for references to names of battles or campaigns. Norman's book contains a place index from which one may discover which regiments gained battle honours. However, not all regiments which fought or served at a particular location received honours, and a more complete list of regiments must be sought at the PRO (Kew) under Monthly Returns (WO 17) or Monthly Returns, Distribution of the Army (WO 73). (Both sets of returns show regiments in numerical order, but WO 73 also includes the distribution of the Army by station.)

Precise details of honours, with dates, full regimental names and Army Order information are contained in Leslie's "Battle Honours of the British and Indian Armies".[46] A very brief summary of campaigns and honours is give in Appendix 1.

Those interested in medals themselves may seek information from many publications by collectors or dealers, for instance Joslin's compilation for Spink & Son.[45]

My Ancestor was in the British Army

In our own search we had started only with the reference to a Norfolk regiment at Waterloo. The list of regiments which fought at Waterloo was found in Dalton's "Waterloo Roll Call",[18] which includes a list of all the officers who fought at Waterloo. In fact there is also Dwelly's published list[26] of all the men and NCOs in the cavalry at Waterloo, but regrettably the same author was unable to complete and publish a corresponding list of infantry before his death. We soon discovered that no "Norfolk" regiment had actually fought at Waterloo, although the 54th (West Norfolk) had been in reserve and the 9th (East Norfolk) arrived after the battle to form part of the army of occupation in France. Here were two possibilities to follow up in the army records at the PRO (Kew). Of course we did not neglect to look in the published cavalry lists, where we found a Sergeant John Watts in the 11th Light Dragoons and a John Watts in the 7th (Queen's Own) Light Dragoons. Neither of these regiments had any strong affiliations with Norfolk, but it was prudent to check the service of both these John Watts at the PRO (Kew) to see if either fitted any of the known facts about our ancestor.

Miscellaneous

Needless to say there are many sources which could lead one to discover the regiment of a soldier ancestor other than the major ones quoted above. Foremost among these must be family papers or recollections, which are always sought by any serious genealogist, however remote the relative or family friend may be.

Local newspapers may be searched near a relevant date, possibly of enlistment, to see which regiments had been recruiting in the area. There is, however, no guarantee that a regiment associated with a particular county was the only one to recruit soldiers in that county.

Two recent indexes of large numbers of army personnel should also be mentioned here. These are Frank Turner's index of Muster Rolls in 1861, and Jim Beckett's index of Chelsea Pensioners discharged between 1806 and 1838. Full details are given on pages 66-67.

To conclude this section, we will summarise the full extent of the information with which we started our own search. There was the oral tradition of an ancestor fighting in a Norfolk regiment at Waterloo. When great-great-grandfather John Watts died at Happisburgh, Norfolk in 1846, the occupation on his death certificate was given as soldier. None of the methods described above had led us to the number or name of his regiment. (Sadly, the Beckett index was not available until 1990). We had to seek John Watts' regiment using army sources at the PRO (Kew). This is the procedure which will be outlined in the next section.

(B) - FINDING THE REGIMENT USING "ARMY SOURCES"

If all "non-army sources" have failed to reveal an ancestor's regiment then the next step must be to visit the Public Record Office at Kew and consult the original army records preserved there. An alternative is to use microform copies, e.g. at Mormon libraries.

The following table lists the possible starting points, roughly in chronological order except that medals and awards have been placed at the head of the list. A commentary and further information follow the table.

WO 100 /	1- 397	Campaign Medals	1793-1912
WO 101 /	1- 7	Meritorious Service Awards	1846-1919
WO 102 /	1- 16	Long Service & Good Conduct Awards	1831-1902
WO 146 /	1- 155	Distinguished Conduct Medal	1855-1909
WO 25 /	1121- 1131	Service Returns No 3, Discharges	1783-1810
WO 25 /	871- 1120	Service Returns No 1	24th June 1806
WO 25 /	1196- 1358	Muster Master Generals' Index of Casualties	1797-1817
WO 25 /	1359- 2410	Casualty Returns	ca 1810-1840
WO 25 /	2411- 2755	Index to Casualty Returns	ca 1810-1840
WO 22 /	1- 300	Royal Hospital Chelsea Pension Returns	1842-1862
WO 23 /	26 - 65	Chelsea Registers of Out-Pensioners	ca 1820-1875

If discharged to pension:-
WO 97 /	1722- 2170	Soldiers' Documents Alphabetical for each of	1873-1882
	1722- 1762	Cavalry	
	1763- 1848	Royal Artillery	
	1849- 1857	Royal Engineers	
	1858- 1870	Foot Guards	
	1871- 2147	Infantry	
	2148- 2170	Corps & Miscellaneous Units	

If not killed in service:-
WO 97 /	2171- 6322	Soldiers' Documents Alphabetical for whole of Army	1883-1913

My Ancestor was in the British Army

The table above comprises the "Army Sources" which one could use on a first visit to the PRO (Kew) if the regiment of a soldier ancestor was still not known. Some words of guidance and warning may be helpful. There is no general index to other ranks prior to 1914. However, some sources are more useful than others as a starting point, and this section is intended to be a guide to them.

The first four sources relate to <u>Medals</u>. Taking the Kandahar example further one can now refer to the series of Campaign Medals in WO 100 to see if the soldier sought was a recipient of the "Kabul to Kandahar Star 1880". Reference to the Class List will show that piece numbers 51 to 53 relate to the Afghan campaign from 1878 to 1880. The Medal Rolls (WO 100, WO 101 and WO 102) are in fact available on microfilm at the PRO (Kew) and also via Mormon libraries. The lists of recipients are arranged by regiment, but a complete search should not be a lengthy task; if the required soldier is not found in these lists, it would still be worth searching the Muster Books and Pay Lists (WO 12 etc) of the regiments present at Kandahar.

The use of the remainder of the table depends very much on the approximate dates when a soldier may have served and on any other clues which one may have accumulated. For the period from about 1783 until 1817 there are three complementary returns under <u>Registers, Various</u> in WO 25, which should cover all soldiers during the time when the British army underwent first a dramatic expansion, then contraction. These are:

<u>Service Returns No 3, Discharges 1783-1810.</u> These contain lists of all soldiers discharged, other than by death or for a casualty, during this period. In the words of the time, they list soldiers who were "discharged between 25 Dec 1783 and 24 June 1806, but were not known to be dead or disqualified from service" i.e. they were possibly available for recall. The attraction of these volumes is that each one refers to several (10 to 20) regiments, so that the whole army is covered by 12 pieces e.g. WO 25 /1125 covers the 1st to 17th Foot. It would certainly be a practical proposition to search the whole army in these lists for soldiers with the required name.

<u>Service Returns No 1.</u> These are a "Statement of the Periods of Service of all the Non-Commissioned Officers, Drummers, Fifers and Privates liable to serve Abroad on 24 June 1806" and as such are virtually an index to the army on that date. If one has some hint of possible regiments in which a soldier may have served, then these returns would be well worth looking at; they would scarcely merit a complete search as they total 250 volumes. There is one piece per battalion with the soldiers listed alphabetically giving their full name, rank and details of service. For example (from WO 25/919 for the 1st Battalion of the 6th Foot):

My Ancestor was in the British Army

Rank	Corporal
Surname	Watts
Christian Names	John
Trades and Places of Birth where more than one of the same Name	-
Date of enlistment in the present Corps	14th April 1796
Former Service in this or other Corps or whole period on the Out-Pension	
Corps or Out-Pension	99th Foot
From	6th March 1793
To	13th April 1796

In each Corps when in more than one, to the 24th June 1806, or half the period on the Out-Pension	99th	3 years 39 days
	6th	10 years 72 days
	Total	13 years 111 days

Entitled to pay for Corporal; served more than 7 but less than 14 years.

Muster Master Generals' Index of Casualties (1797-1817). These contain lists of all soldiers rendered ineffective due to casualty during this period; there is usually one piece per battalion within which soldiers are arranged alphabetically giving the date and place of casualty. Of course in the army the term "casualty" referred to anyone who had ceased to be present for whatever reason; death, going missing or being invalided were obvious reasons but being transferred to another battalion or regiment, being promoted or demoted were also reasons for inclusion in these lists. An example taken from those for the 6th Foot (1st Battalion to 1817, 2nd Battalion to 1815) in WO 25/1227 contains:

Names		Casualties		
Watts, Hugh	[Pte]	Dischd	24 Nov	[1800]
Watts, Willm	[Pte]	Struck off	24 Sept	1802
Watts, Jno	C[orp]	Fm 1o	31 July	[1805]
		To 1o	1 Sept	1807
Watts, John	[Pte]	To 2 Battn	25 July	1813
Watts, John	[Pte]	To Out Pension	16 Aug	[1816]

Continuing these three indexes, which apply predominantly for the duration of the Napoleonic conflicts, a series of Casualty Returns is available for the period ca 1810 to ca 1840. Again the task of searching the Returns is made easier by the provision of an index, but even the latter contains 345 pieces and it would only be worth a lengthy search if one was quite certain that a soldier had served during this time and had not been discharged to pension.

My Ancestor was in the British Army

If a soldier was discharged to pension during the nineteenth century then any of the three remaining sets of documents listed at the end of the above table may be utilised in an attempt to find the regiment in which he served. These are the Pension Returns (for the Royal Hospital Chelsea) (WO 22), Chelsea Registers of Out-Pensioners (contained in WO 23) and Soldiers' Documents (WO 97).

Pension Returns (WO 22) exist for the whole of the British Isles for 1842 to 1862. At first sight this may not appear to be a promising period for investigation, but the arrangement of these Pension Returns makes them particularly useful. They were the means by which we found the regiment of our soldier ancestor John Watts.

The key to their use is that they are arranged by Pension District. Prior to 1842 it would appear that soldiers' pensions were distributed by local officials; 1842 saw the institution of the army's own system of payment in 59 districts in England, 2 in Wales, 12 in Scotland and 33 in Ireland. Thus, if one knows the part of the country in which a soldier ancestor lived, then reference to that area's Pension Returns may well be worthwhile.

The Returns are not records of regular payments to pensioners. A soldier will be found in these so-called Pension Returns - broadly speaking - if he transferred to or from a District, if he was a new out-pensioner, if the pension rate was changed in any way, or if pensions ceased due to death or felony, during the stated period.

It can be seen therefore that these returns could include Peninsula and Waterloo veterans, many of whom would survive to - and then die during - that period, as well as the Crimea pensioners who were discharged to pension in the 1850s.

An example is given below of an entry in one of the sections of the Pension Returns, that for the Norwich District, 1842-1852 (WO 22/76). This was the appropriate district for the village of Happisburgh, on the north-east coast of Norfolk, where our suspected soldier ancestor John Watts lived. After much searching we had finally confirmed that he had been a soldier and we had now discovered which regiment he had served in.

Quarterly Return for Outpensioners of Chelsea Hospital
for 1 October to 31 December 1846

VI Pensions ceased by death

Regt	Rate of pension	Rate of poundage	Rank and name of pensioner	Pension Permt. or Tempy.	Date of Decease	Age at Decease
6	1/1	5	John Watts	Permt.	1 Novr.	76

My Ancestor was in the British Army

These Pension Returns must be considered a major potential source for the determination of a soldier's regiment and it is therefore worthwhile listing the centres at which pensions were paid. There are usually two volumes, each covering a ten-year period for each district.

Returns are available for all centres for both periods 1842-1852 and 1852-1862, unless indicated by
(1) = Returns for 1842-1852 only, or by
(2) = Returns for 1852-1862 only.

England
Bath; Birmingham; Bolton; Brighton; Bristol; Cambridge; Canterbury; Carlisle; Chatham; Chester; Coventry; Deptford; Derby; Durham(1); Exeter; Falmouth; Gloucester; Halifax; Hull; Ipswich; Leeds; Leicester; Lincoln; Liverpool 1st, 2nd(2); London 1st East, 2nd East, 3rd East(2), 1st West, 2nd West, 1st North, 2nd North, South, Woolwich; Lynn; Manchester 1st, 2nd; Newcastle; Northampton; Norwich; Nottingham; Oxford; Plymouth 1st, 2nd, 3rd(2); Portsmouth 1st, 2nd; Preston; Salisbury; Salop; Sheffield; Southampton; Stafford; Stockport; Taunton; Trowbridge; Wolverhampton; Worcester; York(2);

Wales
West; East;

Scotland
Aberdeen; Ayr(2); Dundee; Edinburgh 1st, 2nd; Glasgow 1st, 2nd; Inverness; Paisley; Perth; Stirling; Thurso;

Ireland
Armagh; Athlone; Ballymena; Belfast 1st, 2nd(2); Birr; Boyle(1); Carlow(1); Cavan; Charlemont; Clonmel(1); Cork 1st, 2nd; Drogheda; Dublin 1st, 2nd; Ennis; Enniskillen; Fermoy; Galway; Kilkenny; Limerick; Londonderry; Longford; Maryborough(1); Monaghan; Newry; Omagh; Roscommon; Sligo; Tralee; Tullamore; Waterford;

Overseas
Canada West(2); Channel Islands(1); Isle of Man(2); Jersey(2); Miscellaneous(2).

There are a few further returns for some Irish centres in 1882-3 and some returns for pensioners on convict ships in 1862-7. For descendants of soldiers who emigrated, there is also a series of returns covering the period 1845 to 1880 for Australia, Bengal, Black Pensions, Bombay, Canada, Cape of Good Hope, Ceylon, Colonies, Consuls, Hanoverian, India Office, Madras, Malta, New South Wales, New Zealand, Nova Scotia, Queensland, Tasmania and Victoria. Fuller details are available in the published Class List[77] and in the comprehensive article by Rosemary Oliver.[22] (She points out that it may not be sufficient to search the volumes for the obvious county town and that pensioners sometimes went to a more convenient place; e.g. to Carlisle from Annan, or to Sheffield from Worksop.)

My Ancestor was in the British Army

If one has not been successful in locating a soldier using the District Pension Returns for the period 1842 to 1862, it may well be that he commenced his pension before 1842 and died after 1862. In this event there is a further series of pension registers which should be searched. These are the Admissions Registers of Chelsea Out-pensioners (WO 23/26-65), which cover the period from about 1820 to 1875. They are arranged by regiment, but each volume contains a list of pensioners for about 10 to 15 regiments for an interval of 10 to 20 years. If all else had failed, it might be practicable to search all 40 pieces of this class. Typically the following information, taken from the Chelsea Hospital Admissions Register, ca 1821-1854, 1st-9th Foot (WO 23/36), would be given:

(6th Foot)	Rate	Date of Admission	Residence	Died
Jno Watts	1/1	16th August 1816	Walsham Norfolk Norwich	1st Nov 1846
Saml Whitcomb	1/1	16th August 1816	London 2nd West	-

Although this Admissions Register is nominally for 1821-1854, it can be seen that earlier admissions had been copied in, presumably to make a current register of surviving pensioners. This feature may be regarded as typical of pension records, in that there are many overlaps and duplications; all possible registers should be searched.

The whole range of Chelsea Registers is described in the "Sources" section of this chapter. It will be shown that the above entry, from WO 23/36, is virtually duplicated in the Chelsea Hospital Regimental Registers, under WO 120/55. As an alternative to WO 23/26-65, it would be equally valid to search WO 120/20-30, for 1806-1838, or WO 120/52-64, which records pensions paid between 1845 and 1854 with additions to 1857 (and deaths noted to 1877). Details of the Beckett index for WO 120/20-30 are given below on page 66.

Finally we reach the period from around 1873 to 1913. The table shows that for the first 10 years, 1873 to 1882, the Soldiers' Documents (WO 97) of all pensioners are arranged alphabetically for each of the main sections of the army: e.g. for cavalry or infantry separately. Hence one can proceed directly to these papers and discover which regiment or unit a soldier belonged to. For the remaining years from 1883 to 1913, the outlook for finding evidence of any soldier not killed in service rises to a near certainty: the Soldier's Documents for the whole army are arranged alphabetically in over 4000 boxes. (Sadly the corresponding papers have not survived for soldiers killed in service.)

(C) SOURCES

In this section the major sources of information about other ranks during the period prior to 1914 are described. It is now assumed that the soldier's regiment is known. The main sources include Soldiers' Documents, Muster Books and Pay Lists, Description Books and Hospital Records for Chelsea and Kilmainham; some guidance is given on Deserters and Courts Martial. The emphasis for these sources will be in relation to the cavalry, foot guards and infantry. A final section summarizes the material available for the artillery, engineers, other corps, militia and volunteers.

Soldiers' Documents (for Royal Hospital, Chelsea)

The so-called <u>Soldiers' Documents (WO 97)</u> for the Royal Hospital at Chelsea are the best starting point for details of a soldier's career. They are believed to have survived, however, only for soldiers who were discharged to pension between 1760 and 1882 or for soldiers who were not killed in service but were discharged between 1883 and 1913. Similar documents for those discharged via the Royal Hospital, Kilmainham near Dublin in Ireland are referred to below. The broad arrangement of the Chelsea Soldiers' Documents is given in the following table.

	Piece Nos	Arrangement	Date of Discharge
WO 97 /	1-1271	By regiment number, then names alpha.	1760-1854
	1272-1721	By regiment in numerical order, then names alphabetical	1855-1872
		Names alphabetical for each of:	
	1722-1760	Cavalry	1873-1882
	1761-1762	Household Cavalry	1873-1882
	1763-1848	Royal Artillery	1873-1882
	1849-1857	Royal Engineers	1873-1882
	1858-1870	Foot Guards	1873-1882
	1871-2147	Infantry	1873-1882
	2148-2171	Various Corps, Rifle Brigade, Local and Miscellaneous Units	1873-1882
	2172-4231	Alphabetical for whole Army	1883-1900
	4232-6322	Alphabetical for whole Army	1900-1913
	6355-6383	Supplementary series	1843-1899
	6323-6354	from misfiled documents	1900-1913
WO 121 /	1- 136	Chelsea Discharge Documents of Pensioners	1787-1813
WO 122 /	1- 14	as WO 121, for Foreigners' Regiments	1816-1817
WO 131 /	1- 44	as WO 121, for Deferred Pensions	1838-1896

Soldiers' Documents comprise discharge and, very often, attestation papers; they usually include details of age, birthplace, trade or occupation on enlistment, physical description, statement of service and reason for discharge to pension. From the 1860s a medical history may well be included and from 1883 the papers usually refer to next-of-kin, wife and children. The amount of information included depends on the date. A typical example of a relatively early document is afforded by that for John Watts, consisting merely of a single folded sheet. (WO 97/286)

| 6th Foot | P John Watts | 31st May (18)16 | (Cover) |

Aged 46   Served 20 4/12}
99th   3 1/12} 23 5/12 (years)

Worn Out   Hasbury Norfolk   A Gardiner

I, John Watts, do acknowledge that I have received all my Clothing, Pay, Arrears of Pay and all Just Demands whatsoever from the time of my enlisting in the Regiment mentioned on the other Side, to this Day of my Discharge In Witness my hand this 24th Day of April 1816.

J Hayes   his
Sergt Major   Jno X Watts
6th Regt   mark

I do hereby Certify that the cause which has rendered it Necessary to Discharge the within Mentioned John Watts as stated on the opposite Side has not been from Vice or Misconduct and that he is not to my Knowledge incapacitated by the Sentence of a General Court Martial from receiving his Pension.

John Fisher   A Campbell
Surgeon 6th Regt   Lt Colonel Com.

(Inside of sheet)

His Majestys 6th (or 1st Warwickshire) Regiment of Foot whereof General Sir George Nugent Bt VGCB is Colonel

These are to Certify that John Watts Private in Capt Jas Thomson's Company in the Regiment aforesaid born in the Parish of Hasbury in or near the Town of Hasbury in the County of Norfolk hath served in this Regiment for the Space of Ten [sic] years and One Hundred and Fourteen Days, as likewise in other Corps according to the following Statement but in consequence of being Worn out, is considered unfit for further Service abroad and is proposed to be Discharged and has been ordered by John Fisher, Surgeon to the 6th Reg Depot that his case may be finally determined on having first received all Just Demands of Pay, Clothing &c from his Entry into the said Regiment to the Date of this Discharge as appears by the Receipt on the back hereof.

My Ancestor was in the British Army

And to prevent any improper use being made of this Discharge, by it falling into other Hands, the following is a Description of the said John Watts. He is about Fortysix Years of Age, is Five Feet Four Inches in Height Grey Hair Hazle Eyes Dark Complexion and by Trade a Gardiner.

Statement of Service

In what Corps	Period From	To	Total Service (all as Private) Years	Days
99th Foot	6th Mar 93	13th Apr 96	3	39
6th Foot	14th Apr 96	5th Aug 1816	10 [sic]	114
		Total	13 [sic]	153

Given under my Hand and Seal of the Regiment at Lillers in France this Twenty fourth Day of April 1816

        A Campbell   Lt Colonel
                      6th Regt

York Depot 5 August 1816
I Certify John Watts is unfit for further Service
            Wm Richs Mo... Surgeon to the ...

Later documents were set out on a variety of printed forms. The Soldiers' Document for Thomas Playford, discharged in 1834, is a seven page printed paper with many more details than given for John Watts. Some extracts are given below: (WO 97/8)

HIS MAJESTY'S SECOND REGIMENT OF LIFE-GUARDS, WHEREOF
THE KING IS COLONEL IN CHIEF
And General the Rt Honbl The Earl Cathcart is Colonel.

No.7 Thomas Playford, Corporal of Horse, BORN in the Parish of Barnbydun in or near the Town of Doncaster in the County of York by trade a Farmer.

ATTESTED for the Second Regiment of Life Guards at London in the County of Middlesex on the 18 Sept 1810 at the age of 18 years.

1st SERVICE

			Years	Days
Enlisted 2nd Life Guards	16 Sept 1810			
2nd Life Guards Private	25 June 1810	8 Augt 1816	6	45
Promoted Corporal of Horse	9 Augt 1816	5 May 1834	17	269
		Waterloo	2	
Total Service up to 5 May 1834			25	314

Served in the Peninsula and on the Continent from November 1812 to July 1814, at the Battle of Vittoria 21 June 1813, on the Continent from May 1815 to February 1816, at the Battle of Waterloo 18 June 1815.

2nd DISABILITY
According to the surgeon's report annexed it appears that this is a case
of disease or disability contracted in and by the service without being
attributable to neglect vice or intemperance and the board concurs in the
opinion of the surgeon.

(Corporal Playford of the 7th Troop has been frequently in the Regimental
Hospital since his period of foreign service for various attacks of
rheumatism and rheumatic gout in the joints apparently contracted by
service and from no intemperance of his own. In consequence he has long
been unfit for the active duties of a dragoon and I consider him to be
unfit for further service of the kind. His conduct in hospital has been
uniformly good.

J D Broughton, Surgeon, 2nd Life Guards, Windsor Cavalry Barracks.)

3rd CHARACTER
The Regimental Board is of the opinion that his conduct has been very good.

4th PAY and CLOTHING
He has received all just Demands from his Entry into the Service, up to
the 5th May 1834.

DESCRIPTION of Thomas Playford at the time of his Discharge
He is 42 years of age, 6 Feet 2 Inches in Height, Dark Hair, Dark Grey
Eyes, Dark Complexion, By Trade a Farmer.

MARCHING ALLOWANCE
None paid.

The Board have verified that his Soldier's Book is correctly balanced and
signed by the Officer commanding his troop, and they further declare, that
they have impartially inquired into, and faithfully reported their opinion
on all the matters brought before them ...

George Greenwood	Lt Col	2nd Life Guards	President
L D Williams	Capt	2nd Life Guards	Member
George Bulkeley	Capt	2nd Life Guards	Member

By the latter half of the 19th century an even more detailed set
of forms will be found for a discharged soldier. A series of 21
questions were put to the recruit before enlistment. No. 2167 George
Watts, who joined the 13th Hussars in May 1883, gave his birthplace
as North Walsham, Norfolk, his age as 21 years, 1 month and 23 days,
and reported a 5 year apprenticeship as a moulder to Messrs Randell
of North Walsham (WO 97/4118). He was examined by a magistrate, by
both civil and army doctors, then by two officers. A physical
description and religious denomination were also recorded on
attestation. A medical history form was compiled on enlistment, scars

and marks were noted and he was re-vaccinated. A further medical
sheet noted ailments and treatment. During his 12 year service, he
appeared to suffer nothing worse than the ague, which kept him in
hospital for 12 days in Malta and for 10 days in South Africa;
quinine effected a complete cure. A Statement of Services form gives
details of "promotions, reductions and casualties". He was sent "to
cells" for 7 days in September 1886; in January 1887 he was held in
confinement awaiting trial, then tried and imprisoned for 28 days.
Finally, his Military History Sheet included Next of Kin: father,
James; brothers (younger), Thomas, Robert and William; sisters,
Blanche, Maud and Ethel.

Soldiers' Documents are clearly one of the most important sources
for the genealogist in search of a soldier ancestor. The desirability
of having a general index of the soldiers listed in them has been
identified by the Friends of the Public Record Office, who are about
to proceed with such a project.[83] At May 1991 the PRO (Kew) has
piece numbers 1 to 1279 of WO 97 available on microfilm.

It is important to mention here a further series of records of
service, which are complementary to those in WO 97. These are the
Royal Hospital Chelsea Discharge Documents of Pensioners (WO 121).
For the period 1787 to 1813, piece numbers 1 to 136 are arranged
chronologically by the date of award of pension. As there is no index
of names, this source would be tried only when one had failed to
locate a soldier in WO 97. From some cross-checking for soldiers in
both WO 97 and WO 121, it seems unlikely that an individual would
appear in both series. An example from WO 121/1 is given below:

HIS MAJESTY'S 23rd REGIMENT OF FOOT (OR ROYAL WELCH FUSILIERS)
WHEREOF MAJOR GENL RD GRENVILLE IS COLONEL.

These are to certify, That the Bearer hereof, William Sample, Private in
Major General Richard Grenville's Company of the aforesaid Regiment, Born
in the Parish of West Kirk in or near the Market Town of Edingburgh in the
County of Midlothian Aged Forty Nine and by Trade a Taylor Hath served
honestly and faithfully in the said Regiment Seven Years and Eight Months;
and Twenty Years and Ten Months in the 26th Regiment; but having been
wounded in the left cheek at the battle of Guildford in North America the
15th March 1781 and being old and worn out in the Service, he is rendered
unfit for further Service and is hereby Discharged, and humbly recommended
as a proper Object of his Majesty's Royal Bounty of CHELSEA HOSPITAL. He
having first received all just Demands of Pay, Clothing, &c, from his
Entry into the said Regiment, to the Date of this Discharge, as appears by
his Receipt on the Back hereof.

Given under my Hand, and the Seal of this Regiment, at Tynemouth Barracks,
this Seventeenth Day of March 1787.

Fredk Mackenzie, Major   Royal Welch Fusiliers
Chas Williamson, Surgeon 23rd Regiment

My Ancestor was in the British Army

Muster Books and Pay Lists

   Musters Books or Pay Lists form probably the most comprehensive series of army document to have been preserved. They must have been a vital source at the time they were compiled, providing a body of evidence about a soldier's existence to which reference could always be made. As for Soldiers' Documents they are arranged by regiment, so prior knowledge of this is necessary before searching. Muster Books, however, will include soldiers not featured in Soldiers' Documents, for instance those killed in service. Moreover, Muster Books can be followed through the whole period of a soldier's service to give much fuller information than the summary contained in the Soldiers' Documents.

   If one has already found a set of Soldiers' Documents for a particular individual, then his dates of enlistment and discharge will be known; if not, but the regiment and approximate dates of service are known, then one must adopt a "lucky dip" technique, say every five years until he is located. Each volume usually covers a single calendar year, although earlier ones often relate to a few years.

   Muster Books and Pay Lists are to be found in seven classes:

WO 10 / 1- 2876	Artillery	1708-1878
WO 11 / 1- 432	Engineers	1816-1878
WO 12 / 1- 13305	General (incl. Cavalry & Infantry)	1732-1878
WO 13 / 1- 4675	Militia and Volunteers	1780-1878
WO 14 / 1- 130	Scutari Depot	1854-1856
WO 15 / 1- 102	Foreign Legions	1854-1856
WO 16 / 1- 3049	New Series (Artillery, Engineers, Cavalry and Infantry)	1878-1898

General Notes:
Service in India is included in all cases, except Artillery and Engineers.
For Artillery, see also WO 54, Ordnance Office Registers and WO 69,
Artillery Records of Service.
For Engineers, see also WO 54, Ordnance Office Registers.
For Militia and Volunteers, see also WO 68, Militia Records and WO 70,
Volunteer and Territorial Records.

   Muster Books provide a monthly record of a regiment, stating where each man was, his pay and allowances and, in a remarks column, details of any transfers between battalions or regiments, periods of sickness, furlough etc. Each rank is separately listed, in descending order of seniority. This detail is given on a quarterly form covering three monthly musters, for all except the earliest dates.

My Ancestor was in the British Army

In addition, at the end of each batch of musters, further forms may be included, noting men who became non-effective; sometimes, for depot musters, details are given of allowances paid to men for their wives and children, to enable them to return to their place of enlistment.

For an individual soldier, therefore, Muster Books can reveal a complete, month by month account of his service. In addition, though, initial and/or final musters for a particular man may well provide his birthplace, trade and place of enlistment.

The following shows the main features of a Muster Roll for the 1st Battalion of the 6th Foot at the end of 1815. (WO 12/2390)

	Pay and additional Allowances					(Table continued below)
	Periods for which Payment has been made: or, where not issued, Periods for which the respective Persons are considered to be entitled thereto					
No Privates	From To		No. of days	Rate per diem	Amount issued £ s d	
912 Watson James	25 Sep	24 Dec	91	6d	2 5 6	
913 Watson James	25 Sep	24 Dec	91	6d	2 5 6	
915 Watts John	17 Dec	24 Dec	8	8d	5 4	
918 Webster Henry	25 Sep	24 Dec	91	-	- - -	
924 West James	25 Sep	24 Dec	91	6d	2 5 6	
925 West James	25 Sep	24 Dec	91	6d	2 5 6	
930 White William	25 Sep	24 Dec	91	8d	3 - 8	
935 Wilde James	25 Sep	24 Dec	91	7d	- - -	
936 Wilde Thomas	25 Sep	24 Dec	91	8d	- - -	

No	Reasons of Absence at the respective Musters			Remarks explanatory of the Reasons of Absence at the Musters... dates of Inlistment &c.
	1st Muster	2nd Muster	3rd Muster	
912	-	-	-	-
913	-	-	-	Trade: Labourer of Nilston
915	-	-	Joined from 2nd Battn	Paid by the Detachment Paymaster at Canterbury to 16 December 1815
918	Missing	Missing	Missing	From 28 February 1814
924	-	-	Duty	-
925	-	-	-	Trade: Stone Mason Warwick
930	-	-	-	-
935	Sick Abst	Sick Abst	Discharged	Chelsea Outpension: 24 February 1815
936	Sick Abst	Sick Abst	Transferred	To the 2nd Garrison Bn 25 April 1815

OTHER RANKS - PRIOR TO 1914

My Ancestor was in the British Army

At the time of this muster for the last quarter of 1815, the 6th Foot, or Warwickshire Regiment, were stationed at Lillers in northern France. The first columns of the Muster Book, which give the number of the company and whether men were entitled to higher pay for periods of service exceeding 7 or 14 years, have been omitted for simplicity. A selection of privates feature in the extract, including John Watts, who had just rejoined the 1st Battalion from the 2nd; he is recorded as having been paid up to the 16th December by the detachment paymaster at Canterbury. The army system ensured that soldiers on the move between units were not paid twice!

It should be noted that the number quoted in this 1815 example was not the regimental number, introduced in the 1830s, which stayed with a man during his time in a regiment. These numbers are merely a sequence for this particular muster. (914, 916 etc are omitted here.) Soldiers were listed either by first letter of their surname or strictly alphabetically. There were two James Watsons and two James Wests, so the occupation of one each of them was included in the Remarks column, in order to distinguish between them.

For John Watts, it was possible to trace his career in the Muster Books of the 99th Foot and the 6th Foot, from 1793 to 1816. Some typical extracts for his service are given below.

Year	From To	Location	Regt	Bn	Company	Rank	No. of days	Rate per diem	Amount issued £ s d	Remarks	Source WO 12/
1794	17/8 30/9	Dublin Barracks	99th	-	-	Pte	-	-	-	-	9784
1796	1/4 30/9	Killinay Co Galway	6th	1	-	Pte	-	-	-	From 99th 14th April	2382
1799	25/6 24/7	Cork	6th	1	Capt Lee	Pte	30	1s	1 10 0	On board ship 18-24 August	
1799	25/7 24/8	Quebec	6th	1	Capt Lee	Pte	-	-	1 7 6		2383
1806 1807	25/12 24/3	Deal Barracks	6th	1	Capt Edwards	Cpl	90	1/5	6 7 6	On furlough 24 days	2387
1807	25/6 1/9	Gibraltar	6th	1	Capt Robertson	Cpl	69	1/2¼	4 3 4¼	To Private 1st Sept	2387
1807	2/9	Gibraltar	6th	1	Capt Robertson	Pte	23	10½d	1 0 1½	From Cpl 2nd Sept	2387
1808	25/6 24/9	In Spain & Portugal	6th	1	No 8	Pte	92	8d	3 1 4	(Rolica 17/8) (Vimiera 21/8)	2388
1808 1809	25/12 24/3	Spain & Aspringe(Kent)	6th	1	No 8	Pte	49 41	6d 1s	4 0 6	(Corunna 16/1) In lieu of beer	2388
1813	1/5 24/3	Jersey	6th	2	No 9	Pte	55	1/2	3 1 2	Transf'd from 1st Battn	2451
1816	25/3 24/4	Camp Neve St Omer	6th	1	No 5	Pte	31	8d	1 0 8	Invalid sent to England	2390

My Ancestor was in the British Army

It can be seen that the Muster Books will provide a very detailed record of an individual soldier's service. However, it is important to correlate this record against a regimental history or against accounts of battles. Three battles, Rolica, Vimiera and Corunna, are noted in brackets in the table above; they were not actually mentioned in the Muster Books, but are readily found in the regimental history of the Warwickshire Regiment. A further point concerns rates of pay, which are clearly somewhat variable in the extracts quoted. As already mentioned, slightly higher rates of pay applied for service exceeding 7 or 14 years. Pay would also vary depending on stoppages (for food or clothing), and whether beer was supplied or not. Note the increase to one shilling a day "in lieu of beer" for the 41 days after arrival in England from the withdrawal at Corunna. Those who check the calculations of total pay for the beginning of 1809 will conclude that the soldier was overpaid by fifteen shillings; there seems to be no ready explanation for this, possibly it was some compensation for the rigours of the campaign.

Depot Musters are also important sources for soldiers not located with the main body of the regiment at any time. For the period 1785 to 1878, there is a good selection of Depot Muster Books in WO 12, piece numbers 12055 to 13288. The coverage is not as complete as for the regimental books, and the depot musters to search must be inferred from gaps in the regimental records for a particular individual, but the results can be very worthwhile. For John Watts, successful searches in Depot Muster Books revealed the following.

Year	From	To	Location of Depot	Remarks	Source WO 12/
1812	25/10	24/12	Cork	Paid by regt paymaster to 24/10 Group of 26 men from 6th Ft 1st Bn quartered at Cork, "turned over to Detachment Paymaster".	12444
1812 1813	25/12	24/3	Cork	John Watts paid 1/2 per day in lieu of beer.	12445
1815	13/11	16/12	Canterbury	Group of 64 men from 6th Ft 1st Bn 10 days on 124 mile march from Winchester to Canterbury.	12208
1816	25/4	24/6	Chatham	Group of 23 men from 6th Ft 1st Bn marched from France via Dover.	12302
1816	25/6	1/8	Chatham	Permitted to find own lodgings.	12302
1816	2/8	16/8	Chelsea	To Out-Pension on 16/8. See detailed notes in text below.	12434

My Ancestor was in the British Army

The Chelsea Depot Muster Book for 1816 included a separate book (sometimes these are bound in at the end of the main Muster Book), providing an "Account of Allowances issued to the Wives and Families of Men discharged at Chelsea on Reduction of the Army in the Year 1816. Agreeably to the existing Regulations" and also "Allowances to Men Discharged". The first account revealed that John Watts had a wife and three children, who were paid a total of £1.5.1 for the 67 mile journey from Chelsea to Ely. A wife qualified for three ha'pence a mile, each child a penny a mile. Soldiers themselves were apparently expected to travel ten miles a day, so John Watts was given a travelling allowance of fivepence a day for seven days, to take him to Ely. (Of course the puzzle remains why they would travel to Ely rather than back to John Watts' home parish of Happisburgh in Norfolk. One must assume that the army rule of paying subsistence to return a soldier to his place of enlistment applied, but it has not been possible to verify that John Watts enlisted at Ely, either from army records or from local Quarter Sessions records or newspapers.)

Muster Books often refer to "Vouchers" or "Reports"; these would probably be useful sources of further information but most seem to have disappeared. For example, at the end of 1815, the Muster Book for the 6th Foot referred to Voucher 91: "a No 1 Report from the Detachment Paymaster at Canterbury showing the period a party from England was paid to". However, the Report no longer exists.

1760 - 1877

The main series of Muster Books which refers to cavalry and infantry from about 1760 until 1877 is found in the 13305 volumes of WO 12. The PRO class list for WO 12 is published.[82] The usual starting date quoted for WO 12 is 1732; however, this date applies only to the 1st Foot Guards, or Grenadiers - Muster Books for 1732 and 1741 survive for them. For the majority of cavalry and infantry units, the normal starting date is 1760.

While the first 10000 volumes of these Muster Books relate to the cavalry and infantry in a numerical sequence, the remaining 3000 or so cover a very wide range of units; these include the African Corps, Army Hospital Corps, Army Service Corps, Canada Fencibles, Canada Rifles, Ceylon Rifle Infantry, Falkland Islands Company, Garrison Battalions, Malta Fencibles, Manx Fencibles, St Helena Regiment, Staff Corps, Veteran Battalions, 1st to 12th West India Regiments and some Garrisons; Foreign Corps then follow, such as Corsican Rangers, Dutch Troops, King's German Legion, De Meuron's (Swiss) Regiment and Watteville's; finally there is a series of musters for depots from Aberdeen to York. As indicated above, the latter should not be neglected as they may well provide some interesting extra information about a soldier when he is not actually based with his regiment.

There are separate classes prior to 1878 for the Muster Books of the Artillery, Engineers, Militia and Volunteers, Scutari Depot and Foreign Legions. (See page 37 and section starting on page 58.) Fuller details of the arrangement of Muster Books for the Artillery and for the Engineers are given in an article by Angela Barlow.[24]

The contents of Muster Books did vary over the period 1760 to 1877 but the major features are as outlined in the examples above. A comprehensive survey of the development of army musters is contained in the article by Angela Barlow[24], using the 47th Foot, or the Lancashire Regiment, as an example. Among the many developments, the following may be mentioned. By 1825, pay is no longer shown for each man. Around 1830, each set of musters changed from the financial year (based on quarter days) to the calendar year. In the 1830s, regimental numbers were given to a man on enlistment. From 1840, the number of forms began to grow - there were forms for soldiers in confinement, soldiers forfeiting pay, lists of effects and credits of soldiers who had died, been taken prisoner or were missing, lists of soldiers' remittances. The latter include some of the earliest references to soldiers' wives, or perhaps mothers. After the Crimean War, forms multiplied further - a possible 48 by 1865 and 59 by 1875. For recruits, place and date of enlistment, as well as age, were now quoted. Full details were provided for discharged men, where they were enlisted, where to reside, with travel for themselves and families, fares and destinations. From about 1870, the roll of the married establishment is included, giving first name of wife, number and ages, but not names, of children, and date of being placed on the roll. There was a fixed number of places on the married roll, so a couple might have to wait some time before a vacancy occurred.

1878 - 1898

The "New Series" of Muster Books and Pay Lists (WO 16) commenced in 1878 and continued the classes WO 10 to WO 13. Thus Artillery, Engineers and Militia, as well as Cavalry and Infantry, are all now included in a single class, namely WO 16. In 1882, and then again in 1888, there were reorganizations of the army; many of the currently accepted names of regiments were established by the Cardwell reforms of 1881. Pairs of infantry regiments were combined to form the two battalions of a single unit, e.g. the East Surrey Regiment was formed in 1881 by the amalgamation of the 31st (Huntingdonshire) Regiment with the 70th (Surrey) Regiment, which then became respectively the 1st and 2nd Battalions of the new Regiment. From 1888, WO 16 comprises Muster Books only, without the associated Pay Lists; also they are arranged in companies and by Regimental District, so that one must obtain the number of this, e.g. from Hart's Army List,[11] before one can gain access to the required Muster Books.

OTHER RANKS - PRIOR TO 1914

My Ancestor was in the British Army

A typical New Series Muster Book contains an extensive range of forms, similar in number and content to those described above for the later years of the period 1760 to 1877. It would be impractical to reproduce full examples of even a selection of them, as the forms themselves have become extremely detailed. The following examples are all taken from the 1877-9 Muster Book and Pay List of the 1st Battalion of the 9th Foot (1st Battalion of the Norfolk Regiment from 1882) (WO 16/1413).

Pay and Allowances are now listed on a standard "Form 2"; this contains basically the same headings as in the Muster Book extract quoted above (page 38). In the list of Privates, there were two John Watson - No 1345 was a labourer from Nottingham while the other, No 1479, was a seaman from Norwich. Both were paid a shilling a day from 1st April to 20th September and then transferred to the 2nd Battalion of the 9th Foot on 21st September. Good conduct pay, usually a penny a day but occasionally up to fivepence per day, was also payable. Ominously, there were now printed columns to allow for entries relating to soldiers in military prison, in civil prison or in hospital; No 1344 James Watson forfeited his pay from 18th May to 11th June owing to imprisonment, the first 6 days being in the prison hospital. (A footnote to Form 2, referring to the Brigade or Regimental No, reads: "when pay is charged for the first time for a non-commissioned officer or soldier transferred from another regiment or corps, his former as well as his present number should be inserted; but the former need not be repeated in subsequent pay lists".)

Allowances to Discharged Soldiers were recorded on "Form 24", being a "Statement of the Amount Paid for Allowances to Discharged Soldiers and their Families to take them Home, together with the Expenses of their Guides and Temporary Allowances to Widows and Children of Deceased Soldiers". On the 7th August 1878, No 4043 Private John Mahoney, who had enlisted at Limerick and intended to reside at Tralee, was discharged together with his wife Mary, and their three children, respectively aged 14 years 5 months, 10 years 2 months and 4 years 1 month. His unit was based at Dublin at his time of discharge so their railway fares to Limerick, £2 3s, were paid, together with one day's family allowance of 2s 4d and Mahoney's allowance on discharge of 20s.

Fines for Drunkenness were recorded on "Form 41A". They were imposed either by order of the commanding officer or by sentence of a court martial; the former dealt in multiples of half-a-crown, while the latter started at £1. No 1160 Private M Tobin was fined 10s by the CO on 29th May 1877, but only 8s 8d had been deducted from his pay before he deserted.

Effects and Credits on "Form 49" provided a list of officers, NCOs and men who had become "casualties"; that is, they were lost to the regiment as a result of death, desertion, capture by the enemy, discharge, transfer or going missing. One of those listed for the

My Ancestor was in the British Army

half-year 1st October 1877 to 31st March 1878 was No 1697 Drummer Charles Newth, born in London, and a musician by trade when he had enlisted on 15th December 1871. He became non-effective at Dublin on 15th December 1877, being discharged to the Army Reserve on completion of his term of service. The form included columns relating to the forwarding of effects and credits to next of kin of missing, captured or deceased soldiers.

The army had always disapproved of marriage, as detracting from a soldier's loyalty, but had authorised a ratio of six women to one hundred men up to the first half of the nineteenth century. This proportion was strictly applied when regiments embarked for foreign service. These "on the strength" wives were actually allowed to live with their husbands, usually in an area screened by blankets at the end of the barrack room, in return for the performance of chores such as cleaning, cooking and mending. "Off the strength" wives received no rations or allowances. By about 1870, the married establishment had been formally set up, with married quarters, although there was still a limit to places.

Those whose marriages had been officially sanctioned were placed on the Roll of the Married Establishment on "Form 58". For example, No 782 Private James Battersby and his wife Johanna had been placed on the married establishment on 5th August 1877; their three children were aged 6 years 6 months, 2 years 2 months and 2 months respectively at the date of the muster in March 1878. In the column provided for changes in the roll, the child's birth on 14th January is noted as well as Private Battersby's death on 26th January. This column was also used to indicate, "when a soldier is placed on the roll, the name of the man whose vacancy he fills". On this particular roll, for instance, No 35 Private Edward McMahon and wife Charlotte were placed on the married establishment on 23rd November 1877, "Vice Ptes Sullivan and Eames discharged". (It would appear that at this date a soldier was admitted to the roll only when two had left).

Description Books

Before the days of photography, it was important for the Army to have a good description of a soldier for various not very flattering reasons; foremost among these was the need to provide a physical description in the event of desertion, as well as helping to prevent re-enlistment for bounty or the prevention of pension frauds. Description Books give a physical description of each soldier, together with his birthplace, trade, service and enlistment details. The books survive mainly for the first part of the 19th century and are generally arranged by initial letter of soldiers' names in regimental volumes. These can be found in a variety of classes:

WO 25 / 266 - 688	Regimental Description Books Cavalry, Infantry, Garrison and Veteran Battalions, Foreign Corps	1756-1878
WO 67 / 1 - 34 WO 68	Depot Description Books includes Militia Description Books	1768-1908
WO 54 / 260 - 309	Royal Artillery Description Books	1749-1863
WO 54 / 310 - 316	Sappers, Miners, Artificers Description Bks	1756-1883
WO 69 / 74 - 80	Royal Artillery Description Books	1773-1876

Some typical examples taken from the Regimental Description Book (compiled 1804-1811) for the 6th Foot (WO 25/329) read:

REGIMENTAL BOOK OF HIS MAJESTY'S 6TH REGIMENT OF FOOT

Names		Watts John	Welsh Thomas	Wilkinson John
Rank		Corpl	Pte	Pte
Size Feet Inches		5' 6"	5' 5"	5' 9"
Age Years		31	30	31
Description	Complxn	fair	fresh	fresh
	Visage	round	-	-
	Eyes	grey	blue	grey
	Hair	brown	brown	black
Where Born	County	Norfolk	Lancaster	Lancaster
	Parish	Yarmouth	Blackburn	Leigh
Trade		Mariner	Weaver	Fisherman
Former Service		2 in 99	-	-
Enlisted	By Whom	Dft fm 99	2 Battn	2 Battn
	Where	Waterford	Gt Baddow	Gt Baddow
	When	14 Apl 96	16 Jun 1806	12 Jun 1806
Casualties	Dead	-	30 May 1811	-
	Deserted	-	-	24 Dec 1806
	Discharged	-	-	-
Observations		-	Prisoner Spain 11 Jan 1809	Returned from desertion 7 Feb 1807

My Ancestor was in the British Army

Hospital Records for Chelsea and Kilmainham

   The Royal Hospital at Chelsea was founded in 1682 and opened in
1692, to provide for wounded and disabled soldiers. The corresponding
dates for the Royal Kilmainham Hospital, Dublin, were 1679 and 1684.
By the early 19th century Chelsea could accommodate about 500
in-pensioners and Kilmainham about 200. The vast majority of eligible
discharged soldiers could not therefore be housed within the
hospitals, but had instead to become "out-pensioners". There were
about 3000 Chelsea Out-Pensioners by 1711 and 20,000 by 1792. The
"out-pensioner" category was thus really a method of payment of
pensions to other ranks, and remained so until 1955, when the Army
Pensions Board took it over. The records of pensioners are not
medical ones but relate rather to granting of a daily pension, based
either on length of service or on disability; the award of such a
payment, however small it might have seemed to the recipient, was
some compensation for his service and/or disability.

Chelsea Hospital

   In addition to the Pension Returns (WO 22) and Soldiers' Documents
(WO 97, WO 121), which have already been described, there are three
main sets of records relating to pensioners. These are the Admission
Books (WO 116 and WO 117), the Regimental Registers (WO 120) and what
may be loosely termed the Chelsea Registers (WO 23). Taken
together, these three classes will provide a summary of a soldier's
service, age, occupation, reason for discharge, rate of pension,
place of birth, and a description. Sometimes an entry will be
annotated with the date of a man's death. Much repetition of material
occurs in these three series. Nowadays it is only possible to guess
at the bureaucratic process which brought them into being, but the
genealogist will always check every possible source for a further
grain of information.

   The Admissions Books (of out-pensioners) are contained in two
classes. Pensions awarded between 1715 and 1882 for disabilities are
in WO 116. Those awarded between 1823 and 1902 for long service are
in WO 117. The entries are arranged chronologically as soldiers were
discharged; as there is no index, the approximate date of discharge
must be known before consulting this series. (Class WO 116 also
includes, in piece numbers 125 to 185, a special series of Admissions
Books for Royal Artillery pensions from 1833 to 1913).

   A typical example is afforded by the following three entries taken
from the Chelsea Hospital Admission Book (Disability) for 21st June
to 27th August 1816 (WO 116/22 fo 126).

My Ancestor was in the British Army

Examination of Invalid Soldiers on Friday the 16th of August 1816

Regiment	6th Foot	6th Foot	6th Foot
Name	Prettibier	Watts	Whitcomb
	Josh	John	Saml
Age	45	46	53
Rank	Private	Private	Private
Service (Years Months)			
(in 6th)	16 10	20 4	20 4
(elsewhere)	10 3(in 60th)	3 1(in 99th)	2 7(in 99th)
Total	27 1	23 5	22 11
Rate per diem	1s 3d	1s 1d	1s 1d
Complaint	Worn Out	Worn Out	Worn Out
Where Born	Quebec	Hasbury	Harlington
	N America	Norfolk	Hounslow Middx
Trade or Occpn	Silversmith	Gardiner	Labourer
Remarks			
Height	5' 5"	5' 4"	5' 4"
Hair	black	grey	dark
Eyes	grey	hazle	grey
Complexion	dark	dark	dark
	Died 6 May		
	1830 Per B 88634		

For quite a considerable period, the Admission Books are divided according to cause of discharge, for either disability (as in the above examples from WO 116) or for long service (WO 117). An example of the latter, taken from WO 117/1, is quoted below.

Examination of the cases of Invalid Soldiers who have claims to Pensions for Service alone, not being discharged in consequence of disability or the effect of Military Service, and admitted on the Pension List of Chelsea Hospital on 13 April 1824.

Sergt Jno McGregor; born Strathspey, [Tomenhout], Banff; age 44; height 5' 10", fair hair, blue eyes, fair complexion; trade, labourer; intended place of residence, Bandon, Cork.

Served as Private	1 year 1 month
Corporal	1 year 2 months
Sergeant	19 years 5 months
Total	27 years 8 months

Pension 2s 1 1/2d per day to commence 12th Mar 1824.

Cause of discharge: appointed Barrack Sergeant at Bandon.
Note: having been appointed Barrack Sergeant, will not be entitled to any pension at present.

For those wishing to check piece numbers before proceeding to the PRO (Kew), parts of the class lists for WO 116 and WO 117 are published in the PRO Lists and Indexes, Supplementary Series, Volume VIII, Part 1.[79] For WO 116, this volume covers up to piece number 154; pieces 1 to 124 relate to the cavalry and infantry from 1715 to 1882, while pieces 125 to 154 refer to the Royal Artillery from 1833 to 1882. Further pieces, 155 to 185, continue the Royal Artillery series to 1913. Volume II of the PRO Guide (see PRO Bibliography) states that the class itself continues to piece number 252 with a closing date of 1913. For WO 117, the List and Index volume covers only the first 36 pieces, for discharges between 1823 and 1882; the remaining pieces, finishing at number 77, take the series to 1902.

Turning to the next records, the <u>Regimental Registers (WO 120)</u>, it should be pointed out that these include two distinct sets of volumes, although the primary arrangement is by regiment. The first 51 pieces cover the years ca 1715 to 1843, in six date bands: ca 1715-1756, ca 1717-1775, ca 1742-1784, ca 1730-1812, ca 1806-1838 and ca 1839-1843 (only this last band is indexed by name within the piece). Within each piece, entries are by regiment, then chronologically. A piece may contain between 10 and 20 regiments. For example WO 120/23 contains entries for the 1st to 13th Foot from ca 1806 to 1838. The entry we found for John Watts, on folio 254 of WO 120/23, is identical to that quoted above (see page 47) from WO 116/22. (The Beckett index, covering WO 120/20-30, is described on page 66.)

The second series contained within WO 120, pieces 52 to 70, provides lists of pensions being paid between 1845 and 1854, with additions to 1857. Admissions before 1845 are arranged by rate of pension, and then a chronological set of entries follows. An example of the brief entry now given is taken from the Regimental Register for the 1st to 9th Foot (WO 120/55 fo 157).

6th Foot

	Rate	Date of Admission	Residence	Died
John Watts	1/1	16th August 1816	Norw[ic]h	1/11/1846 E42.662/59

Finally the <u>Chelsea Registers (WO 23)</u> will be described more fully - pieces 26 to 65 have already been mentioned on page 31 as a possible regimental finding aid. It will be noted that the example just quoted above, from WO 120/55, virtually duplicates that from WO 23/36 given on page 31. Clearly the clerks at the Chelsea Hospital and those keeping regimental records shared and noted the same information.

"Chelsea Registers, &c" (WO 23) contain much that duplicates the two series already discussed (Admission Books and Regimental

Registers), but also house unique and unusual sources. The table below summarises the material available in WO 23. Piece numbers 26 to 65 form the main sequence which duplicates much of WO 120; each piece contains a list of pensioners for about 10 to 15 regiments for a period of about 10 to 20 years. However it should be noted that WO 23 continues beyond WO 120 with two further date bands, for 1855-1865 and 1865-1875. The class list as far as piece number 123 is published in PRO List and Index No XXVIII.[77]

WO 23 /		
1- 16	Reports as to invalids admitted to pension (Duplicates some material in WO 116 and WO 117)	1830-1844
17- 23	Returns of East India Company's Pensioners	1814-1868
24	Returns of Greenwich Hospital Naval Pensions	1868-1870
25	Register of Pensions to Militia and Yeomanry	1821-1829
26- 45	"Chelsea Registers" (see notes above)	1820-1854
46- 55	"Chelsea Registers"	1855-1865
56- 65	"Chelsea Registers"	1865-1875
(66-123	Relates to Officers and Widows - see page 14)	
124-131	In-pensioners - Muster Rolls	1702-1789
132	In-pensioners - Muster Rolls	1864-1865
134	List of in-pensioners	1795-1813
135	Pensioners from the King's German Legion	1801-1815
136-140	Pensions being paid in 1806	pre 1806
141-145	Ordnance pensions being paid in 1834	pre 1834
146	Alphabetical register of in-pensioners	1837-1872
147-152	Admission books for pensions payable in colonies	1817-1875
153-159	Lists, registers and admission books of negro and Cape Corps pensioners	1837-1879
160	Admission book of native and colonial pensioners	1880-1903
162-172	Admission books and rolls for in-pensioners	1824-
174-180	arranged chronologically	1917
173	Index to in-pensioners admitted	1858-1933

There is clearly a wide range of information available in these Chelsea Registers. The extracts below are from WO 23/136, the first of four books recording pensions being paid in 1806.

Name		Tarleton Jno	Postleworth Wm
Regiment		6th Foot	6th Foot
Age	Years	79	87
Service	Years	3	21
Admitted (to pension)		1 Apr 1747	30 Jun 1767
Complaint		Lameness in the Hip	Worn Out
Residence		Kirkby Stephen Westmorland	Cartmel Lancashire

My Ancestor was in the British Army

Before concluding the section on Chelsea Pension records, a brief mention must be made of three other sets of out-pension records: the <u>Chelsea Discharge Documents of Pensioners (WO 121)</u>, <u>Chelsea Discharge Documents of Pensioners, Foreigners' Regiments (WO 122)</u> and <u>Chelsea Documents of Pensioners Awarded Deferred Pensions (WO 131)</u>.

Some of the Discharge Documents in WO 121 were introduced in the section on Soldiers' Documents (see page 36), where it was suggested that WO 121 (pieces 1 to 136) must be searched in preference to the Soldiers' Documents in WO 97 for men discharged in the 18th century. For instance, WO 121/1 includes the following for Private Donald MacDonald.

Discharged 18th June 1787
H M 74th Regt of Foot whereof Col John Campbell is Colonel

Donald MacDonald, private in Capt Grant's Company. Born Kilmanivack, in or near the Market Town of Fort William County of Inverness aged 39 years a labourer served near seven years but by an over-exertion in drawing Cannon at the siege of Charlestown and other very fatiguing service at that time, he contracted a violent pain in his breast and spitting of blood, by the continuance of which and consequent long sickness, that has made him very dull of hearing, he is rendered incapable of working and therefore he is hereby discharged and humbly recommended as a proper Object of his Majesty's Royal Bounty of CHELSEA HOSPITAL

Edinburgh 28th March 1787   John Campbell Col late 74th Regt

However, a search in the appropriate part of WO 97 (piece number 861 for the 74th Foot) failed to reveal this Donald MacDonald; there were of course several others of the same name in this Highland Regiment - these included a blacksmith born 1790 at Portrea, a wright born 1801 at Inverness and a gardener born 1806 at Armadale. They were not discharged until the years 1829, 1840 and 1849 respectively.

WO 121 comprises 257 volumes, covering the period 1782 to 1887. The first 136 pieces form the chronological series from 1787 to 1813, already referred to. (These pieces are listed in reference 78). Pieces 137 to 222 are certificates of service in invalid and veteran battalions, 1782 to 1833; a check in these is well worth while if a soldier has not been found in other series of discharge document. Pieces 223 to 257 form a general register of discharges, from 1871 to 1884.

WO 122 covers discharges from Foreigners' Regiments, 1816-1817, in 14 pieces. WO 131 is an alphabetical sequence of those awarded deferred pensions, between 1838 and 1896, in 44 volumes. Both classes are also listed in reference 79.

My Ancestor was in the British Army

Kilmainham Hospital

Kilmainham Hospital was opened in 1684 and catered for Army pensioners in Ireland. It has recently been renovated and opened to the public as the Irish Museum of Modern Art (see Sunday Times, 26th May 1991, page 5.9). The records of Kilmainham Hospital, which are contained in classes WO 118 and WO 119, are unfortunately not nearly so extensive as the material for Chelsea. (The class lists are published in reference 78.)

Kilmainham Admission Books (WO 118), 1759-1863, are similar to those already described for Chelsea (WO 116, see page 47), and cover both in- and out-pensioners. In 1807 existing pensions were re-assessed and these documents became a regular series from that date. Pieces 36, 37, 38, 42 and 43 are entry books of pensioners, containing dates of admission and sometimes death; they are arranged chronologically by date of award of the pension. Piece 13 is a register of pensioners resident abroad who were transferred to the establishment at Chelsea.

The following example is taken from the Admission Book for 24 Feb 1819 to 27 June 1821 (WO 118/42).

Soldiers Admitted 27 Oct 1819

					Years	Days
Regiment	7th Foot	Service				
Name	John Eyers	Marines	20 Oct 1796	13 Jan 1815	18	86
Age	46	7th Foot	28 Aug 1815	22 Oct 1819	4	56
Rank	Private	Total			22	142

Rate	1s 1d per day	Where Born	Marshgibbon Bucks
Complaint	Worn Out	Trade	Labourer
Height	5' 9 3/4"		
Hair	Brown		
Eyes	Grey	DD (Discharged Dead) : 26/6/39	
Complexion	Swarthy	D 29477	

Pieces 39 to 41 and 44 (of WO 118) provide an index to these registers and also to the Kilmainham Discharge Documents of Pensioners (WO 119), 1783-1822.

Thus consulting WO 118/44, which indexes admissions between 24 Feb 1819 and 13 Nov 1822, by initial letters, one discovers that both Dr(ummer) James Watts (Discharge Number B 2427) and Pte Michl McMahon (Discharge Number B 2425) had served in the 49th Foot. These entries could then be followed up in the Admission Books themselves or in the Discharge Documents (WO 119), which give much fuller information. The Discharge Numbers can be used to refer to the class

list for WO 119 and select piece number 63 to obtain the full
entries. These read (WO 119/63):

Discharge Number	B 2425	B 2427
Name	Michl McMahon	James Watt (sic)
Rank	Private	Drummer
Born Parish of	Dicente	Kinsale
Near town of	Ennis	Kinsale
County of	Clare	Cork
Enlisted for	49th Regt	49th Regt
at	Cavan	Jamaica
County of	Cavan	W Indies
on	6 Jan 1808	25 Aug 1795
at (age of)	19	14
Served	13 years 223 days	25 years 357 days
	to 16 Aug 1821	to 16 Aug 1821
Discharged	Reduction of the	Reduction of the
due to	Establishment and	Establishment and
	pulmonary complaints	weakly state of health
Conduct	Good	Good
Age	32	40
Height	5' 8 1/4"	5' 6"
Hair	Black	Black
Eyes	Grey	Hazel
Complexion	Fair	Dark
Occupation	Labourer	Labourer
At	Waterford	Waterford
On	16 Aug 1821	16 Aug 1821
Paid	12s to take him	12s to take him
	to Dublin	to Dublin

Prize Records

A soldier may well have qualified for a share in war prize won in
military action. The details will be found in the Royal Hospital
Chelsea, Prize Records, (WO 164), 1720-1899. These include lists of
entitlement from 1779 to 1858, as well as records of unclaimed shares
and of payments made to claimants or their agents. The volumes are
arranged by action, then by regiment or detachment. Once a soldier's
career is known in some detail, a check can be made against
particular actions for prize money. For John Watts, the only such
bonus was found for the action on the island of Walcheren in 1809
(WO 164/197):

Prize Money for WALCHEREN 1809

6th Foot   (Countersigned)
WATTS, John Private 18s 6 3/4d   21 Oct 1812   John Campbell

My Ancestor was in the British Army

Deserters

If one has evidence, perhaps from Muster Rolls or Casualty Returns, that a man deserted, there are a number of places where this can be followed up. The sources discussed here are Returns of Deserters, Hue and Cry, Newspapers and Bounty Certificates.

Returns for Deserters are to be found in WO 25/2906-2961 and cover the period from 1811 to 1851. (These also include "Returns of the Prisoners on the Savoy Hulk" from 1799 to 1823.) Generally each piece covers a number of regiments (between 10 and 30) for a number of years; it would be feasible to search a set of these returns if one had definite evidence of desertion from a particular regiment or around a certain date. A typical entry, taken from the Returns of Deserters for the 1st Life Guards - 20th Foot, 1826-1834, (WO 25/2910) reads:

6th Foot
Taylor, John, age 28, 5' 8" tall, fresh complexion, brown hair, hazel eyes, deserted 11 Aug 1828 at Canterbury, enlisted 20 Oct 1826 at Manchester; no of report from Regt: 1000; how disposed of: 14701 24 July 1829. Remarks: Second Time.

An even fuller description was given in the "Police Gazette" or "Hue and Cry". The following examples are from HO 75/11.

Issue No	1091	1146
Date	30 June 1838	9 Jan 1839
Name	George Fish	George Pratt
Office No	6338	8116
Corps	80th Foot	68th Foot
Parish (birth)	Massingham	Stoke
County	Norfolk	Warwick
Trade	Labourer	Ribbon Weaver
Age	20	22 1/2
Size	5' 6 1/2"	5' 8"
Person	w made	v stout
Face	round	round
Eyes	hazel	grey
Nose	prop	prop
Hair	lt brown	brown
Arms	prop	prop
Legs	stout	stout
Mouth	prop	prop
Marks and)	recruit; passed	large mole on left arm;
Remarks)	the surgeon	seen on way to Cork
Time	20 June	28 Dec
Place	Stamford	Spike Island
Coat	baragan	red fatigue
Trousers	baragan	reg cloth

My Ancestor was in the British Army

"Hue and Cry", which was published on Wednesdays and Saturdays, was distributed to all police stations to aid in the apprehension of deserters and other criminals. Copies are available at the PRO (Kew) for 1828 to 1845 in HO 75. A large table at the end of each issue contains details of some 50 - 60 "Deserters from Her Majesty's Service". Lists of deserters from British units in Australia and New Zealand have also been published.[55][56] (See page 77.)

Deserters were often mentioned in advertisements in local newspapers, in attempts to secure their recapture. One must of course know the date of desertion from some other source to make it worth while searching, unless the newspaper has been fully indexed. The "Bury and Norwich Post" for 6th March 1793 carried the following advertisement, which is typical; although the Suffolk Militia was based at Hilsea, near Portsmouth, the missing men were all from East Anglia.

HILSEA BARRACKS Feb 9 1793   WESTERN REGIMENT of SUFFOLK MILITIA
Commanded by Colonel the Earl of EUSTON

Deserted from the above Regiment the under-mentioned men: Whoever will apprehend and lodge them in any of his Majesty's goals (sic), shall receive TWENTY SHILLINGS reward for each man, by giving sufficient proof of their apprehension and confinement, to John Spink Esq., Bury St. Edmund's, or the Commanding Officer of the Regiment at Hilsea. T BLOMFIELD, Capt and Adjt.

> WM. PULFORD, aged 22, 5 feet 9 inches high, light brown complexion, light brown hair, grey eyes, by trade a labourer, place of abode, Needham Market, and serving for William Worlidge, Creeting St. Peter.
> STEPH. RANSON, aged 22, 5 feet 5 in. high, light brown complexion, light brown hair, grey eyes, by trade a blacksmith, place of abode, Shimpling, and serving for George Keddington, Stanningfield.
> WM. TINGAY, 5 feet 8 1/2 inches high, fresh complexion, light brown hair, grey eyes, place of abode, Brandon, and serving for himself.
> WM. SMITH, 5 feet 8 inches high, pale complexion, sandy hair, dark eyes, by trade a woolcomber, and serving for Robert Hawkins, Hadley.
> JOHN JACKSON, 5 feet 7 inches high, dark complexion, black hair, dark eyes, by trade a labourer, and serving for Wm. Cuthbert, Bildeston.

Deserter bounty certificates were found among the Exchequer Land Tax records in class E 182 by Goulden.[91] These are certificates of arrest of deserters from the army and militia, with orders from magistrates for bounty to be paid to those responsible for arrests. A card index, at the PRO (Kew), covers London and Middlesex from 1783 to 1814, and other counties are being added.

My Ancestor was in the British Army

Courts Martial

As in civilian life, further information will be available about an ancestor if he got into trouble. In the 18th century and early part of the 19th centuries, discipline was of course harsh and was intended to be exemplary so that flogging was the standard punishment; later in the 19th century, fines and penal servitude were substituted. For a soldier who committed a minor offence, discipline was exercised by his Company Commander, while more serious cases would come before his Commanding Officer. He could then be tried by a District Court Martial or by a General Court Martial, depending on the severity of the offence. The surviving series of court martial records have all passed through the office of the Judge Advocate General. Full details of this office and of the features of the various courts martial are contained in the PRO Information Leaflet Number 84.[84]

The records which survive from the Judge Advocate General's office relate to four types of court martial: General Court Martial, Field General Court Martial, General Regimental Court Martial and the District or Garrison Court Martial. A General Court Martial was the only court which could deal with commissioned officers, but also handled serious cases concerning NCOs and other ranks. A Field General Court Martial dealt with most cases which arose overseas during wartime. A General Regimental Court Martial could try only NCOs and other ranks, and could not deal with capital offences; it was abolished and succeeded by the district court martial in 1829. The District or Garrison Court Martial handled lesser offences committed by NCOs or other ranks; it could not pass sentence of death, transportation or floggings of more than 150 lashes.

The verdicts and sentences of courts martial were subject to confirmation, mitigation or remission by higher authority. For instance, a decision overseas to cashier a commissioned officer required the personal confirmation of the sovereign; other decisions might be confirmed by an area commander-in-chief or by the general officer commanding. Eventually records of all courts martial reached the office of the Judge Advocate General - except for a Regimental Court Martial, whose proceedings should have been retained by the regiment.

Courts martial for commissioned officers are readily found, as they could only be tried by General Court Martial. The three types of record which relate to individual trials are papers, proceedings and registers. Papers were written during the court martial and forwarded to the office of the Judge Advocate General, where volumes of proceedings were generated, together with registers, which provide a tabular summary. Selected records relevant to a search for the court martial of an officer are listed below; for brevity, the title "Judge Advocate General's Office" has been omitted from each line. It should be remembered that many records in these classes are closed for 75 years.

WO 93 /	1- 68	Miscellaneous Records	1650-1969
		1A is an index to WO 91 and WO 92	
		1B is an index to trials of officers	1806-1904
WO 71 /	1-1359	Courts Martial Proceedings	1668-1977
	121- 342	Papers, in date order	1668-1850
	13- 33	Proceedings, entry books, home	1692-1796
	34- 64	Proceedings, entry books, home & abroad	1715-1790
	65- 98	Proceedings, entry books, marching regiments	1756-1789
WO 91 /	1- 51	General Courts Martial confirmed at home	1806-1904
		Proceedings, continuation of series in WO 71	
WO 90 /	1- 9	General Courts Martial Abroad	1779-1960
		Registers of CM confirmed abroad	
WO 92 /	1- 10	General Courts Martial	1666-1960
		Registers of CM confirmed at home	
WO 89 /	1- 5	General Courts Martial	1666-1829
		Duplicates much of WO 92, includes	
		full proceedings for 1666-1698 and 1759-60	
		summaries only for 1812-1829	

Examples of entries found, for the 6th Foot, in the Register of General Courts Martial Abroad, are as follows (WO 90/1):

Name	Purcell John	Roach Wm	Sayers John
Rank	Ensign	Private	Private
At	Gibraltar	Gibraltar	Almeida
Date	4 Aug 1807	4 Jan 1808	3 Nov 1808
Offence	Being drunk on guard	Neglect of duty etc	Absenting himself from his regt housebreaking etc
Sentence	Hon(ourabl)y Acq(uitte)d	1000 lashes Remitted	To be hanged

It can be seen from these extracts that both officers and other ranks could be tried by a General Court Martial. NCOs and other ranks could also be tried by General Regimental Court Martial (before 1829) or District Court Martial (after 1829). Thus searches for the trial of NCOs or other ranks must be made in more than one set of records. In the case of General Courts Martial, the procedure is as described above for officers; one may find papers, proceedings and registers. However, for General Regimental Courts Martial, only registers have survived, for 1812-1829, in WO 89, while for District Courts Martial, the surviving registers, in WO 86, span 1829 to 1971. The following

table summarises the material, which should be searched for NCOs and
other ranks, in addition to the General Court Martial records noted
in the previous table.

WO 89 /	1- 5	General Courts Martial	1666-1829
		includes general regimental courts martial	1812-1829
		confirmed at home and abroad	
WO 86 /	1-122	District Courts Martial	1829-1971
		registers, confirmed at home and abroad	
WO 87 /	1	District Courts Martial, London	1865-1875
WO 88 /	1- 7	District Courts Martial, India	1878-1945

In our own researches for John Watts, we had found, from Muster
Rolls, that he was reduced from corporal to private at Gibraltar on
1st September 1807. Accordingly we consulted WO 90/1 for General
Courts Martial Abroad, 1796-1825, WO 91/2 for General Courts Martial
confirmed at home (July 1807 to September 1808), and finally WO
71/210 for General Court Martial papers, (July to September 1807),
but without success. Presumably his offence had been dealt with by
normal regimental discipline.

The papers for the court martial of Ensign John Purcell were
available in WO 71/210. Although evidence was given there by several
soldiers of the 6th Foot, we did not find any reference to John
Watts. The death sentence on Private John Sayers was confirmed by Sir
John Moore, as noted by Fortescue.[6]

The next day he (Moore) entered Almeida, where an unpleasant duty awaited
him. The Sixth Foot, which had occupied the town since the evacuation of
the French, was suffering from the misrule of a bad commanding officer,
and was in a disgraceful state. The officers had been negligent; the
conduct of the men had been infamous, and one private was actually under
sentence of death by court-martial. Moore confirmed the sentence, and then
called the real culprits - the officers - before him... He now addressed
the officers of the Sixth with great severity, told them that they were
unworthy to go on active service, and passed on them the hardest sentence
which he could inflict - that he should leave them behind... The fact
must therefore be recorded, not from any malignancy towards a regiment
which has long since recovered and enhanced its fair fame, but in justice
to a great commander.

This episode casts an interesting light on the regiment in which an
ancestor served and leaves one wondering whether Private John Sayers
deserved his fate.

Artillery, Engineers, Other Corps, Militia, and Volunteers

Most soldiers will have been found in the two largest categories of the army, namely cavalry or infantry (including foot guards). However, there were and are several other major groups in which fighting men have served. These include artillery, engineers and other corps, militia and many categories of volunteers. Each group merits a chapter, if not a book, but there is only space here to summarise records which exist exclusively for them.

Artillery

The Royal Regiment of Artillery, formed in 1722, (together with the Royal Engineers, formed in 1716 but not actually "Royal" until 1787), were separate from the rest of the Army, being under the Board of Ordnance and not the War Office, until 1855. The Royal Horse Artillery was founded in 1793. In 1899 there was a reorganisation of the Royal Artillery, which formed two separate branches, the Royal Horse and Royal Field Artillery, and the Royal Garrison Artillery. A single corps was formed in 1924, although the Royal Horse Artillery retained its title and distinctive badge. A full history of the Board of Ordnance is contained in PRO Information Leaflet 67.[84] Extensive records exist exclusively for soldiers in the artillery and are summarised in the table below. (Note that Soldiers' Documents for the Royal Artillery are arranged alphabetically for each of the three periods between 1760 and 1882.)

WO 10 /	1-2876	Artillery Muster Books and Pay Lists	1708-1878
WO 54 /	1- 948	Ordnance Office Registers	1594-1871
	260- 309	Royal Artillery Description Books	1749-1859
	317- 328	Artillery Discharges, Transfers & Casualties	1740-1859
	338- 481	Registers of Artillery Pensions	1816-1840
	672- 755	Artillery Miscellaneous Pay Lists	1692-1860
WO 69 /	1- 905	Artillery Records of Services etc.	1756-1911
		includes records of service for RA	1791-1855
		and records of service for RHA	1803-1863
	63- 73	Registers of Baptisms and Marriages, RHA	1859-1877
	74- 80	Description Books	1773-1876
	551- 582	Registers of Baptisms and Marriages, RA	1860-1877
	583- 597	Registers of deceased soldiers (& 644-646)	1821-1873
	779- 782	Indexes and posting books for Artillery	
	801- 839	records of service in WO 69	
WO 97 /	1210-1271	Soldiers' Documents - Royal Artillery	1760-1854
	1306-1358	Soldiers' Documents - Royal Artillery	1855-1872
	1763-1848	Soldiers' Documents - Royal Artillery	1873-1882
WO 116/	125- 154	Chelsea Admissions Books (Disability) RA	1833-1882

My Ancestor was in the British Army

Engineers

The Corps of Royal Engineers grew from an officer corps of engineers, established by the Board of Ordnance in 1716, and a corps of Royal Military Artificers (non-commissioned ranks), formed in 1787. The title of the Royal Artificers was changed in 1813 to Royal Sappers and Miners, which led eventually to the "Sappers" nickname, by which the Royal Engineers are known. When the Board of Ordnance was abolished in 1855, the two corps, like the Artillery, were placed under the War Office. The two separate corps of officers and other ranks were then merged into a single Corps of Royal Engineers in 1856. The RE dealt with military aviation, then with aircraft, until the formation in 1912 of the Royal Flying Corps. Similarly the RE Signal Service was the precursor of the Royal Corps of Signals, formed in 1920.

The following records apply exclusively to engineers. As for the artillery, Muster Books and Pay Lists continue from 1878 to 1898 in the new series of WO 16. (see page 37)

```
WO 11 /      1-  432   Engineers Muster Books and Pay Lists      1816-1878

WO 12 /                Muster Books and Pay Lists
             10916     Military Artificers                       1798
             13291     Sappers and Miners -                      1831-1832
             13292     Discharges without Pension                1833

WO 54 /      1-  948   Ordnance Office Registers                 1594-1871
           310-  316   Description Books for Sappers,            1756-1833
                       Miners and Artificers
           329-  337   Engineers Discharges, Transfers, Casualties 1800-1859
           482         Returns of Sappers and Miners             1830
                       entitled to pension

WO 97 / 1148- 1152     Soldiers' Documents - Corps of Sappers    1760-1854
        1359- 1364     Soldiers' Documents - Royal Engineers     1855-1872
        1849- 1857     Soldiers' Documents - Royal Engineers     1873-1882
```

Other Corps

Beside the two senior corps, the artillery and the engineers, of the pre-1914 army, there were numerous other corps, most of which have undergone several changes of title. A detailed study cannot be given here and the reader is referred to Brereton's authoritative guide[4] for historical information and for order of precedence. (The Royal Armoured Corps is omitted here, having been formed in 1939 from mechanised units of the Cavalry of the Line and the former Royal Tank Corps.)

My Ancestor was in the British Army

Corps which existed in some form before 1914 are mentioned briefly below, in order of precedence of their present-day successors. The following table then gives information about individual soldiers' records, which are unfortunately not nearly as extensive as for soldiers already discussed.

The Royal Corps of Signals (formed 1920) derived from the Royal Engineers Signal Service. The Royal Army Chaplains' Department (1919) originated with the department formed under a Chaplain-General in 1796. The Royal Corps of Transport (1965) has a complex family tree, among its progenitors being the Commissary General (pre 1794) under Treasury control, Royal Waggon Corps (1799), Royal Waggon Train (1802), Land Transport Corps (1855), Military Train (1856), and the Army Service Corps (1869), which became Royal in 1918.

The Royal Army Medical Corps (1898) sprang from the Medical Staff Corps (1855), Army Hospital Corps (1857), Army Medical Staff (1873) and once more the Medical Staff Corps in 1884. The Royal Army Ordnance Corps (1918) has a pedigree stretching back, like those of the artillery and engineers, to the Board of Ordnance. (The RAOC took over the RASC supply tasks in 1965.) Field Train (1792), Military Store (1857), and Ordnance Store are among the many titles of earlier units.

The Corps of Royal Military Police (1926) had its origins in the Provost-Marshal and the Provost Service. The Military Mounted Police (1855/1877) were followed by Military Foot Police (1885), combining into a single corps in 1926. The Royal Army Pay Corps (1920) derived from civilian clerks in the 17th century (forerunners of agents such as Cox's) and from commissioned Paymasters with the rank of Captain. By 1893, soldier-clerks assisted these officers in the Army Pay Corps, briefly joined by a Corps of Military Accountants (1919-1925).

The Royal Army Veterinary Corps (1918) started as the Army Veterinary Department (1881). From about 1796 qualified "vets" had been appointed to each cavalry regiment by the Head of the School of Veterinary Medicine in London. The Royal Military Academy Sandhurst Band Corps (1923/1947) descended from a band at Sandhurst in 1815; with no more than 39 members, it could claim to be the smallest corps in the British Army.

The Small Arms School Corps (1919) derived from the School of Musketry at Hythe in Kent (1854). The Military Provost Staff Corps (1906) started life in 1901 as the Military Prison Staff Corps. The Royal Army Educational Corps (1946) was preceded by a Corps of Army Schoolmasters (1846) and an Army Educational Corps (1920). The Army Physical Training Corps (1940) followed the Army Gymnastic Staff (1860) and the Army Physical Training Staff (1918).

Lastly we come to Queen Alexandra's Royal Army Nursing Corps (1949), which derived from the Army Nursing Service (1881), and followed the legendary work of Florence Nightingale in the Crimea.

My Ancestor was in the British Army

Queen Alexandra was patron of Queen Alexandra's Imperial Military Nursing Service (1902), amalgamated with the Territorial Army Nursing Service (1907) in 1949. (The authors' aunt, Major Phyllis Heymann, served in both QAIMNS and QARANC; we would have been intrigued to hear her response to Brereton's statement[5] that QARANC are "of course nurses rather than soldiers"!)

The relatively small number of records available at the PRO (Kew) for various corps are summarised in the following table.

WO 12 /		Muster Books and Pay Lists	
	1522- 1535	Royal Wagon Train	1799-1833
	1536	Staff Corps Cavalry	1813-1818
	10365-10451	Army Hospital Corps	1860-1876
	10453-10490	Army Service Corps	1870-1878
	10655-10681	Commissariat Staff and Transport Corps	1860-1870
	10823-10834	Land Transport Corps	1855-1856
	10910-10915	Medical Staff Corps	1855-1861
	10917-10943	Military Labourers (mostly Mauritius)	1837-1875
	10947-11015	Military Train and Horse Transport	1856-1870
	11065-11090	Staff Corps	1799-1837
	12970-	Depots - School of Musketry - Hythe	1854-1878
	-12996	Depots - School of Musketry - Fleetwood	1861-1867
WO 16 /		Muster Books and Pay Lists (New Series)	1878-1898
WO 25 /	233- 258	Chaplains, Payments and Certs of Service	1805-1843
	582- 602	Military Train Description Books	1857-1869
WO 67 /	32	Commissariat Staff Depot Description Book	1859-1868
	33- 34	Military Train Depot Description Books	1837-1868
WO 97 /		Soldiers' Documents	
	1153	Wagon Train	1760-1854
	1174- 1177	Royal Staff Corps	1760-1854
	1183	Corps of Military Labourers	1760-1854
	1698	Army Hospital Corps	1855-1872
	1702	Land Transport, Army Hospital and Medical Staff Corps	1855-1872
	1703- 1704	Military Train	1855-1872
	1720- 1721	Military Labourers, Commissariat Staff Corps, Military Store Staff Corps and School of Musketry	1855-1872
	2148- 2153	Army Service Corps	1873-1882
	2154- 2156	Army Hospital Corps	1873-1882
	2157	Military Staff Corps	1873-1882
	2170	Corps of Armourers, Military Labourers, School of Musketry	1873-1882
	2171	Military Mounted Police	1873-1882
WO 111 /	1- 13	Army Ordnance Corps	1901-1919

OTHER RANKS - PRIOR TO 1914

My Ancestor was in the British Army

Militia

Militia, the oldest of English auxiliary forces, should properly be the subject of a complete book. Dr I Beckett's study of the British auxiliary forces, including the militia, volunteers and yeomanry, gives a full account of their development.[30] Two booklets published by the Federation of Family History Societies provide detailed coverage of muster rolls and militia on a county by county basis, noting material in the Public Record Office, in numerous county record offices as well as in other locations. These are Gibson and Dell's "Tudor and Stuart Muster Rolls"[27] and Gibson and Medlycott's "Militia Lists and Musters, 1757-1876".[28] (The earliest rolls for militia, 1522-1640, held at the PRO (Chancery Lane) are also described in PRO Information Leaflet 46.[84])

Able-bodied men aged over 16 had long been required to do military service, usually in their own shires or counties. In an emergency, these men would be available as soldiers. In Tudor times, trained bands were organised at the parish expense. Militia were much more strongly established by an Act of 1757, following the Seven Years' War; extensive records listing men were created, and exist for the whole period until 1829, when the militia ballot was suspended. Voluntary enlistment continued through the nineteenth century, leading to the formation of a Special Reserve, the Territorial Force or Army, just before the first World War.

For the Tudor and Stuart period, the introduction to the booklet by Gibson and Dell[27] gives the historical basis of the Muster Rolls and Militia Lists. The earliest rolls date from 1522, when Wolsey ordered a muster, which may be seen as a pretext for a detailed valuation of property. The arrangement of documents is by parish within the hundred. Extensive lists exist for the period up to 1580 (with a few further examples up to 1640) in several classes of both Exchequer records and of State Papers Domestic. It should be noted that all these records are located at Chancery Lane not at Kew. They predate the main period of interest of this booklet, and full information should be sought in the above reference.

For the period of resurgence of the militia, from 1757 onwards, the introduction to the booklet by Gibson and Medlycott[28] provides a detailed survey of the several types of list produced. As Medlycott pointed out in an earlier article entitled "Some Georgian 'Censuses'",[29] the militia ballot lists (1757-1831) and the "defence" lists (1798-1804) form a group of records which may be said to take the place of censuses; clearly they should be consulted by every genealogist, once the parish of origin has been determined, and not just by those tracing a military ancestor.

By the time of the Napoleonic conflicts, Britain was maintaining a constitutional home defence force, the militia, which could not be sent out of the country; a militiaman who joined the regular army was liable at this time to six months' imprisonment.[25] By the Ballot

My Ancestor was in the British Army

Act of 1802 most men aged between 18 and 40 could be drafted into the militia. If there were insufficient volunteers in an area, lists were compiled of able-bodied males, following which ballots were held to select some of them for service. Those selected, if unwilling to serve, but able to pay a fine of £15, could buy immunity for five years. Alternatively, if they could find a substitute, they could acquire immunity for life; the initial going rate was £25. It is important to distinguish between the initial lists - called Militia Ballot Lists by Gibson and Medlycott (but often called Militia Lists in other sources) - and the lists which followed the ballot, termed Militia Muster Rolls or Enrolment Lists.

An example of a militia enrolment list, dated 23rd October 1779, shows that men were sworn for the Westmorland Militia at Appleby. William Whitehead, a taylor aged 17, height 5' 5", born at Orton, was serving for Robert Bowman of Orton. On the other hand, Thomas Nelson, a cooper aged 18, born at Ravenstonedale, was serving on his own behalf for that parish. Some even volunteered, such as Thomas Gibbins, a cooper aged 21, born at Scattergate, who served for the village of Hoff.[31] These examples are from the Lonsdale papers at the Cumbria Record Office, Carlisle, and are typical of many such lists which are available at County Record Offices, either in Lieutenancy papers or in private collections.

Very similar to the earlier militia ballot lists are what Medlycott has called "Defence Lists". This term covers the Posse Comitatus lists of 1798 and the Levee en Masse lists of 1803-4. With the very real threat of invasion in early Napoleonic times, orders were given to compile lists of men not already serving in any military capacity. Again, these lists would be sought for the relevant area by any genealogist, not just one interested in a particular military ancestor.

An example of the value of such lists is afforded by the publication of the Levee en Masse for 1803 for Staincliffe with Ewcross Wapentake in the West Riding of Yorkshire, under the title "The Craven Muster Roll 1803".[32] We were interested in the Willan family in the Dent Township of Sedbergh Parish, and the males aged between seventeen and fifty-five could be identified. John Willan, a labourer, was in class 1, unmarried men under thirty with no child living under ten years of age. George Willan, a farmer, was in class 2, unmarried men between thirty and forty-nine with no child living under ten years of age. Thomas Willan, a labourer, was in class 3, married men between seventeen and twenty-nine with not more than two children living under ten. Another John Willan, labourer, was in class 4, others not included in the first three classes.

As well as the units mentioned above, an Army of Reserve was raised by the Additional Forces Act of 1803, in an attempt to increase recruitment into the regular army. This reserve was raised by ballot in the same way as the militia. There was never conscription as such, but considerable pressure was now brought to

bear on those in the ranks of the militia and the reserve to transfer
to the regular army. An interesting commentary on this complicated
area is contained in Glover's "Wellington's Army".[25]

The families of men who served in this Army of Reserve were
entitled to a "Family Allowance" of 1s 6d per week for the wife and
for each child under ten years of age. The records of these payments
are contained in the Exchequer Receivers' Accounts of Land and
Assessed Taxes, Subsidiary Documents (E 182) at the PRO (Chancery
Lane). A most interesting article on the accounts for the
Basingstoke area of Hampshire has been published by Edward Lawes.[33]
For example, one of the 42 families listed for Stockbridge in May
1804 was that of James and Eleanor Gornall, with their children
Eleanor 8, Ann 4, Philip 3, William 1. (E 182/922, Part 2.)

It is worth noting, while discussing E 182, that this class
contains deserter bounty certificates for militia, as well as for the
regular forces (see page 54). Goulden[91] also points out the
availability of some early court martial books for militia in WO 68.
These are 1st Tower Hamlets Militia, 1813-1825 (WO 68/420); North
York Militia, 1793-1855 (WO 68/195-7); Hampshire Militia, 1729-1808
(WO 68/380).

From 1759 to 1925, many further militia records are kept at the
PRO (Kew); documents such as muster rolls, description books,
enrolment books, returns of officers' service, are available. The
major sources are listed in the table below. It must be noted,
however, that much material relating to the militia was never
collected centrally and should be sought in County Record Offices and
private collections.

WO 13 /	1-4675	Muster Books and Pay Lists Militia, including Supplementary Militia and Local Militia, Fencible Infantry and Cavalry, Yeomanry, Irish Yeomanry and Volunteers	1780-1878
WO 68 /	1- 568	Militia Records including enrolment books, description books, casualty books, court martial books	1759-1825
WO 96 /	1-1522	Militia Attestation Papers	1806-1915

Volunteers and other Auxiliary Forces

Volunteer groups had of course arisen at various times in the
history of the country, usually when invasion threatened. They
consisted of infantry (or Rifle Volunteers) and cavalry (or
Yeomanry). Most units disappeared after Waterloo, were reformed in
the 1850s and at the time of the Boer War, but were all incorporated
into the Territorial Force in 1908.

OTHER RANKS - PRIOR TO 1914

Fencible infantry and cavalry were regular regiments raised for service at home but were often classed with the militia. When the army was reorganized on a regional basis in 1882, many county militia regiments and volunteer units became third, fourth and even fifth battalions of local regiments.

The expression "auxiliary forces" means the militia, the yeomanry and the volunteers; this definition is given in the Army Discipline and Regulation Act, 1879. At a time when the pay and allowances for the regular land forces, at home and abroad, totalled nearly £5 million, it is interesting to note the following expenditure on auxiliary and reserve forces:

	£
Militia, not exceeding 132,526 men including 30,000 militia reserve	495,200
Yeomanry cavalry	47,900
Volunteer corps	512,400
Army reserve first class, not exceeding 22,000 and army reserve second class	203,000

Beckett's study of the British auxiliary forces[30] has been mentioned in the section above. A social and political history of the volunteer force has been written by Cunningham.[34] Holding[39] also provides a useful introduction to the topic of volunteers and auxiliary forces. The following table presents a list of material available at the PRO (Kew).

WO 13 /	1-4675	Muster Books and Pay Lists Militia, including Supplementary Militia and Local Militia, Fencible Infantry and Cavalry, Yeomanry, Irish Yeomanry and Volunteers	1780-1878
WO 97 /	1091-1112	Soldiers' Documents Local Regiments (Militia) - (arranged alphabetically by name of soldier)	1760-1854
	1173	Fencible Volunteers	1760-1854
WO 127/	1- 23	South African War, Local Armed Forces Nominal Rolls	1899-1902
WO 128/	1- 165	Imperial Yeomanry Soldiers' Documents, South African War (Index in WO 129)	1899-1902
WO 129/	1- 12	Imperial Yeomanry Registers South African War	1899-1902

OTHER RANKS - PRIOR TO 1914

OTHER SOURCES — PRIOR TO 1914

There are of course many other sources of information on officers and other ranks outside the War Office classes in the Public Record Office at Kew. Some of these are outlined in this section for the period preceding 1914. The topics covered are: Army Indexes, the Waterloo Committee, Museums, Medals and the Army Medal Office, Vital Records, Archives Abroad, London Gazette, Indian Armies and the Journal of the Society for Army Historical Research.

ARMY INDEXES

The task of making an index of soldiers, even for a limited time-span, is clearly a daunting one in view of the very large numbers involved. Two major indexing projects are described below - these are the Beckett index of Chelsea Pensioners, 1806-1838, and the Turner index for 1861.

For those who do not know the regiment of a soldier discharged during the period 1806-1838, there is an important new finding aid. This is an index to eleven pieces of the Regimental Registers of Chelsea Pensioners (WO 120/20-30); all infantry regiments, Guards and cavalry (but not artillery) have been included in an index of about 82,000 names. Copies have been deposited at the PRO (Kew), at the Society of Genealogists and at the Manchester & Lancashire FHS Library. Microfiche copies are on sale from the Manchester and Lancashire Society; alternatively enquiries should be made to the organiser and editor, Mr J D Beckett, 34 Eastwood Avenue, Droylsden, Manchester M35 6BJ.

The index gave the following entries for John and Robert Watts:

Year	Name	Age	Regiment	Birthplace	County
1818	Watts Jn	34	3FG	Wantage	Brk
1826	Watts Jn	40	1FG	Blakesley	Nth
1814	Watts Jn	25	94	Chippenham	Wil
1816	Watts Jn	46	6	Hasbury	Nfk
1808	Watts Jn	49	7	Cawley	Gls
1820	Watts Jn	37	22	Paisley	Rfw
1811	Watts Jn	22	14	Hardington	Nth
1816	Watts Jn	34	47	Bethnal Green	Lnd
1820	Watts Jn	38	7DR	Berkeley	Gls
1820	Watts Jn	27	7DR	Pentonville	Mdx
1817	Watts Robt	42	80	Tyrone	
1812	Watts Robt	36	2FG	Trowbridge	Wil
1806	Watts Robt		92		
1817	Watts Robt	37	1DG	Holstead	Lei

My Ancestor was in the British Army

The Turner Index covers all soldiers from the rank of Sergeant-Major downwards, for the April-June quarter of 1861, corresponding to the 1861 Census. (Of course, the only soldiers who would feature in the 1861 Census would be those located in barracks in the UK.) The index gives number, rank and regiment for every name listed in the Muster Rolls and Pay Lists, that is, in WO 12, the general pay lists, in WO 11, RE pay lists, and also WO 10, RA pay lists. Officers are adequately covered by Army Lists. An appendix gives where the regiment was stationed and its depot. The July 1862 lists for men of the 19th-21st Dragoons and of the 101st-109th Foot have also been included; the first pay lists of these regiments do not start (excluding the early 19th century lists) until July 1862. (These regiments were formed from men who were serving with the East India Company's European regiments, before the British Government took over direct control of India following the mutiny.)

The compiler of the "Army, Other Ranks, April-June 1861" index is Mr F B Turner, 27 Kings Barn Lane, Steyning, West Sussex BN44 3YR, who welcomes inquiries. It is best to write first for a quotation as the number of names supplied can be variable. A total of about 200,000 men are included in this index.

In our own searches, it seemed interesting to see if either of John Watts' sons, Robert and John, had followed him into the army. The list provided by Frank Turner was as follows.

Name		Regiment			Number	Rank
Watts	Jno	4th Light Dragoons			92	
	John	3rd Light Dragoons			175	
	John	4th Light Dragoons			1506	Orderly Room Clerk
	John	Scots Guards			365	
	John	3rd Ft	1st Bn		3409	Cpl
	John	4th Ft	2nd Bn		1106	
	John	7th Ft	1st Bn	(Depot)	2428	C/Serg
	John	21st Ft	1st Bn	(Depot)	327	
	John	21st Ft	2nd Bn		951	
	John	23rd Ft	1st Bn		4397	
	John	23rd Ft	1st Bn		5369	
	John	41st Ft			4094	
	Jno	86th Ft			287	
	John	87th Ft			3399/712	
	John	96th Ft	(Depot)		477	Drummer/Fifer
	John	101st Ft			1130	
	John	York Recruiting Depot			----	Recruit (for RA)
	Robert	6th Ft	1st Bn		1569	C/Serg
	Robert	57th Ft	(Depot)		2212	

A "National Soldiers' Index" is being developed by Jim Beckett, (address on page 66), for the period 1792 to 1872, but primarily

OTHER SOURCES - PRIOR TO 1914

pre-1852. It includes names of soldiers from sources such as parish records, monumental inscriptions, transcriptions of barrack census returns, medal lists or from newspapers and other printed references. Contributions from such sources or from personal researches would be gratefully acknowledged; requests for searches in the index should of course be accompanied by a donation. (An index to soldiers who served in the Crimea is being compiled from muster rolls and medal rolls by Major (retd) Brian Oldham, who will publicise it when ready in the Genealogists' Magazine - probably early 1993.)

Further specialised indexes are mentioned in two publications of the Federation of Family History Societies. These are the "Marriage, Census and other Indexes for Family Historians"[96] and the "Unpublished Personal Name Indexes in Record Offices and Libraries".[97] Addresses of compilers and terms of access can be obtained from these sources. Typical projects include "Napoleon's British Prisoners 1803-1813" by Madame M Audin; "Light Brigade - all participants and survivors of the Charge" by Ken Horton; "Regiments Census Index, 1861 to 1891" by H J C Holyer and a "Military Index of Wales" by Mr J B Rowlands. Many short lists of regional interest have been published and a selection is given under references 98-104.

WATERLOO COMMITTEE

The Waterloo Committee was founded in 1973 by His Grace the Duke of Wellington and is a charitable trust with a Belgian counterpart in Brussels. Its objects are "to promote public education and appreciation of the Battle of Waterloo, to preserve and restore the site of the battle, to encourage research on all matters pertaining to the campaign and to establish a more accurate historical representation at Waterloo of the events of the 15th June 1815 and thereafter".

There is an Association of Friends, whose Chairman, Derek Saunders, has compiled an index of all the men who served in the British Army - and in the King's German Legion - at Waterloo. (Application to join the Association, which publishes a Journal, should be made to the Secretary, Gordon E Robinson, 16 Ruskin Road, Willingdon, Eastbourne, Sussex; the annual subscription is £7.) The computerised index may be consulted for a search fee of £5, which goes towards restoration of the battlefield. The compiler does request that those enquiring should have carried out substantial research of their own, or be reasonably certain of their case, before approaching him. He has set up a Waterloo Museum at Broadstairs. (Address: Mr D P Saunders, Waterloo Museum, 4 Crow Hill, Broadstairs, Kent CT10 1HN.)

We enquired, on behalf of a friend researching the name Bradbury in Marsden, West Yorkshire, about soldiers with that name who fought at Waterloo. Family tradition and letters recorded that two Bradbury

My Ancestor was in the British Army

brothers had lost their lives in the service of their country, one in the last charge of the French at Waterloo. Derek Saunders sent the following details:

Bradbury	Daniel	Driver	Royal Horse Artillery G Troop
Bradbury	Emmanuel	Sergeant	1st Dragoon Guards Wallace's No 3 Troop
Bradbury	Francis	Private	2nd Life Guards
Bradbury	George	Private	1st Dragoon Guards Elton's No 1 Troop
Bradbury	John	Private	1st Dragoon Guards Elton's No 1 Troop
			Killed in action 18th June
Bradbury	Randle	Private	52nd Foot
Bradbury	Thomas	Private	33rd Foot No 3 Company
			Wounded 18th June
Bradbury	William	Private	15th Light Dragoons

ARMY MUSEUMS

Although it is unlikely that one will find material relating to a particular soldier ancestor in an Army Museum, it is certain that one can find many interesting documents and equipment, which should bring to life the conditions which he faced. There is one National Army Museum (primarily for the period preceding 1914) but there are probably in excess of a hundred Regimental Museums.

The National Army Museum, Royal Hospital Road, London SW3 4HT, houses the national collection of British army relics and "the story of the British soldier through five centuries". There is also a Reading Room where books, archives, photographs and prints relating to the history of the British, Indian and colonial armies may be consulted. Material is generally indexed by regiment, but there are also biographical indexes to books and archives. The collection is extensive and varied; the following items were among many in an exhibition ("Only a Scrap of Paper?") held there in 1986.

Regimental Hospital Register	19th Foot	1789
Regimental Punishment Register	Monmouth and Brecon Militia	1793
Payments to relatives of Officers and Men killed	87th Regt	July 1807 to April 1814
Roll of Soldiers' Families	9th Queen's Royal Lancers	Oct 1906

The National Army Museum has agreed to house an important series of documents, previously held by the Ministry of Defence, relating to deceased soldiers' effects. These records cover the period 1901-1921 for other ranks and 1901-1929 for officers. It must be emphasised that this material is NOT currently available for use by researchers. When it has been catalogued, a further notice will appear in the Genealogists' Magazine. (See earlier note, 23(9), 338, Mar 1991.)

OTHER SOURCES - PRIOR TO 1914

My Ancestor was in the British Army

The records of deceased soldiers' effects are particularly valuable as they cover soldiers killed in service during 1901-1913; the main material for this period, Soldiers' Documents (WO 97), only relates to discharged soldiers. The record books contain useful genealogical information; the name and relationship of recipients of a deceased soldier's estate are given, as well as service details, such as unit, regiment, rank and regimental number.

Record No	661911	Account & Date	London 6/18
Registry No	E/616225/1	Credits	£19-5-10
Soldier's Name	Watts, Reginald	Charges	£19-5-10
Regt	25 Bn MGC	Account & Date	MO 8/18
Rank No	Pt 143035	Date of Authority	21-8-18, 26-11-19
Place and	France, Action	To whom authorised	Fa: Henry G
Date of Death	21-3-18	Amount Authorised	£19-5-10, 9s 10d

Regimental Museums are often located in those cities and towns traditionally associated with particular units e.g. the Royal Warwickshire Regiment Museum at St John's House, Warwick. However, with the Cardwell reforms in 1881 and then the defence reductions of 1968, one must not expect to find a museum for every single old regiment e.g. the former 43rd (Monmouthshire Light Infantry) and the 52nd (Oxfordshire Light Infantry), together with the 60th (King's Royal Rifle Corps) are all incorporated in the Royal Green Jackets, whose collections and history are displayed at Peninsula Barracks, Winchester. A full list of Army Museums with details of access may be found in Terence Wise's "Guide to Military Museums"[53] or in the current issue of "Museums and Art Galleries in Great Britain and Ireland", which has a section on Services Museums.

There is no known listing of documents (prior to 1914) held by regimental museums and headquarters. A full description of soldiers is included in an enlistment book, 1881-1903, for the Lancashire Fusiliers, (Royal Regiment of Fusiliers, Wellington Barracks, Bury) and a similar nominal roll for the 80th Foot, 1804-1881, is at the Staffordshire Regiment RHQ, (Whittington Barracks, Lichfield).

MEDALS and the ARMY MEDAL OFFICE

Medals have been mentioned above (see page 24) in the context of the search for the regiment of a soldier ancestor. Once a soldier's service is known, it is tempting to see if he received a campaign or service medal. He may even have received one of the more famous medals for gallantry or for meritorious service.

The primary sources for medal awards are the medal rolls at the PRO (Kew).[84] Campaign medal rolls are in WO 100; a summary of the relevant campaigns is given in Appendix 1. Meritorious Service Awards are in WO 101/1-7, for the period 1846 to 1919; Long Service and Good Conduct Awards are in WO 102/1-16 for 1831 to 1902.

My Ancestor was in the British Army

Awards for individual gallantry date from the Crimean War. Published books list recipients of the more famous, the VC, DSO and DCM.[48][51] The original records at the PRO (Kew) are in WO 98 for the VC; WO 32 for the DSO and MC; WO 146 for the DCM - recipients of this award, from 1855 to 1909, are also listed in reference 79.

The Army Medal Office is located at Government Office Buildings, Droitwich, Worcestershire WR9 8AU, and it administers the award of Honours, Decorations and Medals for the Ministry of Defence. The possibility exists of next of kin claiming such awards on behalf of deceased soldiers, but the regulations are stringent. (The Army Medal Office will supply a Statutory Declaration Form and an Explanatory Note on Unissued Awards to Deceased Personnel.) An interesting account has been given by Andrew Skingley, who successfully claimed the Queen's South Africa Medal (1899-1902) on behalf of his great-uncle No 5727 Pte Charles Lodge of the 1st Essex Regiment.[52]

There are two separate cases to consider; the first is when medals were not actually issued (or were returned to the Medal Office), the second applies to the replacement of awards that have been lost. The medal rolls at the PRO (Kew) are the source which must be checked to see if an ancestor was entitled to an award. The following advice from the Army Medal Office then applies:

"If a person's name appears on a Medal Roll it must be accepted that the medal was not only awarded but also issued. When the medals have been issued in respect of deceased servicemen, it is usual that the name and relationship of the recipient is shown against the name of the person who earned it. Likewise, if the medal was not issued or if it was returned as not delivered to the earner, an appropriate endorsement would have been made on the Rolls."

"Honours, Decorations and Medals that have been awarded or earned by deceased persons but have not been presented or issued, may be claimed by the Legal Beneficiary or the Next of Kin without restriction."

The legal beneficiary of the deceased's will would of course be his executor(s); if there was no will then any medals could be claimed by the next of kin in a prescribed order. The phrase "without restriction" implies that there is no time limit for such claims. (It would appear, however, that the Military General Service Medal 1793-1814, cannot be claimed.[95])

There are limits, however, to claims for the replacement of awards. "The replacement of Honours, Decorations and Medals that have been irrevocably lost can be approved as a pre-payment issue to the person to whom they were awarded or, if deceased, to those persons entitled to claim initial awards; in this case, however, approval will not be given if the claimant is beyond the first generation".

OTHER SOURCES - PRIOR TO 1914

My Ancestor was in the British Army

"VITAL RECORDS"

Family historians will of course follow up the traditional lines of research, in church and civil registers, in the UK and abroad. These records are vast and, even when partially indexed, do not usually give a direct lead to soldier ancestors. Some useful pointers are given, to encourage searchers not to give up.

Registers of Baptisms, Marriages and Burials

Soldiers travelled the world as part of their experience of life in the army; this did not stop them from getting married or having children, despite the many limitations imposed by the army when they were on active service overseas. Mention has already been made above (see page 21) of the usefulness of army records of birth, marriage and death in tracing a soldier's regiment. However, it is clear that the military made much use of civilian churches wherever the army of the time happened to be. Once one knows where an ancestor served then it is logical to check on the parish registers of nearby churches to see if any records are available of his family. (A first check would of course be made in the relevant sections of the International Genealogical Index.)

A notable collection of soldiers' marriages is Michael Burchall's "Sussex Military Marriages 1750-1812",[104] covering 86 parishes. Peyton's index covers stray military marriages in Cornwall.[99] In Tiverton, Devon, Sheila Pike noticed that many marriages of soldiers took place at St Peter's and she extracted 65 such events just for the years 1795-1800.[23] For example:

```
James Cumming      Sergt      62nd Foot      St Catherines  Edinburgh
Mary Lee                                     Of this parish
17 Oct 1798  by licence


Andrew Townsend    Soldier    11th Foot      Ealms  Co Derry
Elizabeth Cornish                            Of this parish
11 Aug 1796  by licence
```

The frustration of searching for a soldier's missing marriage can only be lessened by hoping that it may turn up one day in a collection of "strays", such as those for Guernsey in the marriage registers of St Helier, Jersey.[98] Two examples are:

```
George Lowe              57th Foot
Martha Berryman                          Of Guernsey
13 Aug 1815


Peter Faddy      Captain  Royal Artillery
Margaret Dutron                          St Peter's Port  Guernsey
16 Sep 1815                              now living in St Helier
```

My Ancestor was in the British Army

Marriage Licence Bonds, which are increasingly being indexed nowadays, may also provide a lead to a soldier's marriage far away from home. This example is from Norwich Archdeaconry bonds for 1813-1837.[86]

```
14 Sep 1818                                (ANW/24/93/35)
(at King's Lynn St Margaret or St Nicholas)
Thomas Fitzgibbon s 33 Sergeant 5th Regiment   Yorkshire   Huddersfield
                             Dragoon Guards
Ann Willoughby     s 30                    King's Lynn  St Margaret


Bondsman:
James Short             Machine Maker      King's Lynn  St Margaret
```

For our own searches, involving Pte John Watts of the 6th Foot, we knew that he had left the army in August 1816 with a wife (first name Catherine) and three children (see page 41). He had presumably married and had these children during his last six or seven years in the army, unless of course he had married the widow of a comrade, as frequently happened, and "acquired" the latter's children. We had searched the IGI and also the indexes to Regimental Registers and Chaplain's Returns without success; the Regimental Registers for the 6th Foot do not survive before 1837 and so the only remaining course was to see whether his marriage or children's baptisms took place in parishes near where he was stationed.

John Watts had served in Canada with the 6th Foot and it proved possible to borrow a microfilm copy of the Register of Holy Trinity Anglican Church, Quebec from the Public Archives of Canada in Ottawa.[61] Many events relate to British soldiers, for example:

11th June 1800
Catherine Firty, daughter of John Firty, Private of the 6th Foot, and Elizabeth, his wife was buried.

26th November 1799
Catherine Smith, daughter of John Smith, Sergeant of the 6th Foot, and Francoise, his wife was baptised.

2nd November 1799
John Egan, age 20, Private of the 6th Foot, died 2 Nov 1799, was buried; present, from 6th Foot, Sgt James Robinson and Cpl Robert Nash.

29th September 1800
Samuel Parks, age 32, Corporal of the 6th Foot, executed for murder 29 Sep 1800, was buried.

John Watts had been based in Gibraltar during 1807-8 so we asked for searches to be made of the appropriate registers there. The

My Ancestor was in the British Army

Military Chapel, or King's Chapel, holds records of baptism from 1769, marriages from 1771 and burials from 1786.[65] An Army Chaplain is still based at King's Chapel and has care of their registers. (We must sadly note that so far there has been no trace of any relevant record either of the marriage of John Watts and Catherine, or of the baptisms of the three children born by 1816.)

At this point it is worth mentioning another potential source of information on the records of births, baptisms, marriages, deaths and burials of "The British Overseas", compiled by Geoffrey Yeo.[74] The important feature of this compilation is that it lists records which are held in the UK. It also provides details of places and dates for two of the following sets of non-statutory registers now at the PRO (Chancery Lane) and covering broadly the period 1826 to 1951:

RG 32 / 1 - 35	Miscellaneous Foreign Returns	1831-1953
RG 33 / 1 - 160	Miscellaneous Foreign Registers & Returns	1627-1958
RG 34 / 1 - 9	Miscellaneous Foreign Marriages	1826-1921
RG 35 / 1 - 69	Miscellaneous Foreign Deaths	1830-1921
RG 36 / 1 - 13	Registers and Returns of Births, Marriages and Deaths in Protectorates of Africa, Asia	1895-1950
RG 43 / 1 - 19	Miscellaneous Foreign Returns of Births, Marriages and Deaths Indexes	1627-1947

Yeo's booklet gives details for RG 33 and RG 36; he also notes that, for entries before 1946, indexes are available at the PRO (Chancery Lane) in RG 43. Details are also given of some Foreign Office registers, held at the PRO (Kew), of births, baptisms, marriages, deaths and burials. These registers formed the basis of consular returns to the Registrar General; it would appear that some material is unique and not duplicated in the Consular Returns now held at St Catherines House.

Yeo refers also to some records of Forces chaplains abroad held at the Guildhall Library, London, namely those for the Cape of Good Hope Garrison, 1795-1803, and for the Gibraltar Garrison, 1807-1812. These are indexed in a composite index of Foreign Registers at the Guildhall. The volume for the Gibraltar Garrison would seem to have been the personal register of one Thomas Tringham, serving as "Chaplain of Brigade to the Forces in Gibraltar" at that time. A typical entry reads

> John Cameron Harvey Wilman, son of Harvey Wilman, Captain in the
> 2nd Battn of the 9th Regiment of Foot, and Abigail his wife, born
> at Warrington, County of Lancaster on the 6th day of January 1810,
> baptised at Gibraltar on the 5th day of April 1812 by me
>
>   Thomas Tringham

The Chaplains' Returns (1796-1880) have been mentioned above (page 23); however, it would seem that there is no certainty that all registers compiled by army chaplains have actually been returned to the appropriate authority and entered with the records currently available at St Catherine's House. For instance, the Archives Nationales du Quebec[64] has the original Garrison Registers for Quebec for 1797-1800 and 1817-1826; the first set related to soldiers of the 24th and 26th Foot, being kept by Rev James Henderson and Rev Alex Spark, while the later registers were the work of Rev Joseph Langley Mills, Chaplain of HM Garrison in Quebec. (These are also available on microfilm from the Public Archives of Canada in Ottawa.) It seems probable that many such records are dispersed in various archives.

Some Garrison Registers, for "events occurring abroad", are indeed kept at St Catherine's House and it is likely that most names from them are indexed in with the main series of Chaplains' Returns. However, since Yeo refers to these Garrison Registers but does not include details, a list of them is provided here:[75]

Garrison and Station Registers (Original Registers) held by the GRO

Garrisons of Cork	Births Baptisms	1886-1910
	Births Baptisms	1913-1914, 1921
Garrison of Cologne	Baptisms	1920-1929
	Marriages	1919-1929
Antwerp and places in Dutch Brabant	Births Baptisms Marriages	1810-1815
Ostend, Martinique and Trinidad	Births Baptisms Marriages Burials	1812-1816
St Jean de Luz and Toulouse (France) and Vera (Spain)	Baptisms Marriages Births Baptisms	1813-1814 1809-1818
Valenciennes (France)	Marriages (two only)	1817
Ionian Islands, Kingdom of Naples and elsewhere	Births Baptisms Marriages Burials	1809-1864
Army of Black Sea and British Salonika Force	Marriages	1916-1923
Garrisons of Egypt	Marriages	1886-1924
Guadaloupe and North America	Bapt Marriages Burials	1813-1815
Madeira	Bapt Marriages Burials	1814
Garrison of St Lucia	Bapt Marriages Burials	1898-1905
Barbados (Windward and Leeward Islands Command)	Deaths Burials	1804-1906
Garrisons of Halifax, Nova Scotia, Quebec, Toronto and Kingston (Upper Canada)	Baptisms) Marriages) Burials)	(1823-1906 (1813-1871 (1847, 1866-69 (1793-1870

At the PRO (Kew), WO 156 (Registers of Baptisms and Banns of Marriages) contains ten pieces. Baptisms are for Dover Castle (1865-1916), Shorncliffe and Hythe (1878-1939), Dover (1929-1940), Buttervant (1917-1922), Fermoy (1920-1921), Jerusalem and Palestine Command (1939-1947) and Sarafand, Palestine (1940-1946). Marriage Banns for Sarafand (1944-1947). Burials for Canterbury Garrison (1808-1811, 1859-1884, 1957-1958).

My Ancestor was in the British Army

Civil Registration etc in the British Isles

The Registrars General in London, Edinburgh, Dublin and Belfast hold a variety of records, including the familiar civil registers, which are of direct relevance to military ancestry.

Soldiers will clearly be mentioned in the normal records of births, marriages and deaths, from 1837 onwards in England and Wales, although there is no specific or separate index to personnel in the armed forces. These records, and the main series of Regimental Registers and Chaplains' Returns kept at St Catherine's House, have been referred to above (pages 17-18, 21-23). Both the latter series include "events which occurred when regiments were stationed in the UK".[75]

It is worth noting that there are records at the General Register Office, Edinburgh, for soldiers of Scottish birth and origin. "Service records (from 1881)" include Army Returns of Births, Deaths and Marriages of Scottish persons at military stations abroad during the period 1881-1959, and certified copies of entries relating to marriages solemnised outside the UK by Army Chaplains since 1892, where one of the parties is described as Scottish and at least one of the parties is serving in HM Forces. "War registers (from 1899)" cover the deaths of Scottish soldiers in the South African War (1899-1902); World War I (1914-1918), the deaths of Scottish persons serving as Warrant Officers, Non-commissioned Officers or Men in the Army or as Petty Officers or Men in the Royal Navy; World War II (1939-1945), incomplete returns of the deaths of Scottish members of the Armed Forces.

The General Register Office, Dublin, has entries, required under the Births, Deaths and Marriages (Army) Act, 1879, of Irish persons serving throughout the British Commonwealth up to 1921. Paul Gorry reports that the index entries are at the back of each normal quarterly index volume. There is also a separate index of deaths of Irish soldiers for the Boer War, 1899-1902.[89]

ARCHIVES and SOURCES ABROAD

Australia

Reference has been made above (page 30) to the War Office Pension Returns (WO 22), which are available at the PRO (Kew) for Australia for the period 1876-1880, New South Wales 1849-1862 then 1871-1880, Queensland, Tasmania and Victoria 1876-1880. There is a complementary set of records in the South Australian Archives for the period July 1843 to December 1844.[54]

There are no major series of original records in Australia of the many soldiers who were in British regiments and corps stationed there. A complete list of these units, with covering dates, is provided by Ronald Montague,[57] together with the location of relevant records. Many muster books and pay lists are available on microfilm in Australian (and New Zealand) National and State Libraries under the Australian Joint Copying Project (AJCP).[58] Further useful guidance on genealogical sources, primarily for Australian soldiers, is contained in a guide published by the Australian War Memorial.[59]

Army Deserters from HM Service in Australia have been transcribed from the Victoria Police Gazette by Yvonne Fitzmaurice.[55] Volume I covers 1853 to 1858; Volume II for 1859 to 1870 also includes deserters in New Zealand. A typical example reads:

Rank	Pte	Enlisted Place	Warrington
Regt No	707	Date	7 7 1855
Name	Joseph Beckton	Birthplace	Manchester Lancs
Age	37 y 4 m	Occupation	Silk-weaver
Height	5' 5"	Regiment	50th
Compx'n	Fresh	Place of Desertion	Sydney
Hair	Sandy	Date of Desertion	19 3 1869
Eyes	Grey	Remarks and Brands	(see VPG = more information available from source or author)

Another publication, listing military and naval deserters in Australia and New Zealand, has been compiled by Rae Sexton.[56]

Canada

Reference has been made above (page 30) to the War Office Pension Returns (WO 22), which are available at the PRO (Kew) for Canada for the period 1845 to 1862, and for Nova Scotia for 1858 to 1880.

The Public Archives of Canada, Ottawa, hold, in Record Group 8, a surprisingly large series of original records relating to the British Army. This Record Group, "British Military, Ordnance and Admiralty Records, 1757-1903", relating of course to activities in Canada, consists of four series. Series I (formerly the "C" Series) comprises British Military Records, Series II covers Ordnance Records. (Series III and IV relate to Admiralty Records). There is a name index to much of the material; this index and Series I have been microfilmed and so may be borrowed for study elsewhere.[62]

In our search for information on John Watts we looked at three volumes of depositions, memorials, returns and correspondence for the 6th Foot.[62] John Watts did not feature in these but many soldiers are named. For example, for the 1st June 1801, there is a return of 15 men, giving names and origins, who had deserted three days earlier; the CO requested permission to try them before a General Court-Martial. 13 were apprehended within the next 10 days, heading for the USA, and it was assumed that the others had probably perished in the woods. On the 19th May 1801, it was reported that Captain Martin Alves and a detachment of the 6th Foot, which had sailed from Portsmouth on the "Sovereign" on the 22nd April, had been shipwrecked on Cape Breton Island; the 20 men, 5 wives and 3 children were all safe but had lost clothes and equipment. Names, ages and heights of men were given, as were the names of the women.

Further military material is available at the Public Archives in various manuscript groups (MGs). MG 13, War Office, London, comprises an extensive collection of copies and microfilm of War Office records kept at the PRO (Kew), selected to relate to activities of the British Army in Canada. MG 18, Military and Naval Documents, includes copies of some Muster Rolls of New England troops serving against the French between 1710 and 1760. (The original rolls are in the Massachusetts Archives, Boston.) MG 23, Late Eighteenth Century Papers, and MG 24, Nineteenth Century Pre-Confederation Papers, both contain interesting military items. For example, there is a record book of punishments ordered by courts martial at the Quebec Garrison between 1777 and 1784. All manuscripts are well calendared by the Public Archives Manuscripts Division.[63]

New Zealand

Reference has been made above (page 30) to the War Office Pension Returns (WO 22), which are available at the PRO (Kew) for New Zealand for the period 1845 to 1854 then for 1875 to 1880. As for Australia, there are no major series of original records in New Zealand of the many British soldiers stationed there. Ronald Montague's book[57] also fully covers New Zealand.

A most useful source for those who suspect that a soldier forebear was discharged in New Zealand has been provided by Hugh and Lyn Hughes.[69] From muster rolls they have transcribed names, and birthplaces where given, of all soldiers of the "Imperial Foot Regiments" who were discharged there between 1840 and 1870. Those involved were foot regiments numbers 12, 14, 18, 40, 43, 50, 57, 58, 65, 68, 70, 80, 96 and 99. Over eight hundred soldiers of the 58th Rutlandshire regiment took a New Zealand discharge.

Five hundred army pensioners recruited from Great Britain settled as the Royal New Zealand Fencibles between 1848 and 1853 at Howick, Otahuhu, Onehunga and Panmure. The names of these military colonists have been extracted from sailing lists and indexed by Shirley Kendall[70] in the "Pensioner Gazette", which records personal accounts of the settlers and their descendants.

USA

The National Archives of the United States hold extensive records of volunteer soldiers who fought in various wars, in the Federal Government's interests. The so-called compiled military service records date from 1775 to 1902, from the Revolutionary War to the Philippine Insurrection. The National Archives Building also houses service records for US Regular Army Officers, 1789-1917, and for enlisted men, 1789-1912. There is clearly very little material available for soldiers who served in the British Army, unless an ancestor changed his allegiance during the revolutionary period.

Those interested in American military records will find a full description in Chapter 8 of Eakle and Cerny's "The Source".[72] A section covers the period of the "colonial wars, 1675-1763", and an extensive bibliography lists published muster rolls from this period. The National Archives' own guide to genealogical research also refers to volunteers' and regular army records.[73]

LONDON GAZETTE

The London Gazette, dating from 1666, is England's oldest surviving newspaper. "Published by Authority", it is the official newspaper of the government, carrying acts of state, proclamations and appointments to offices under the Crown in its weekly editions and extensive supplements. Full series may be found in the State Papers Room of the British Library, at the PRO (Kew) in ZJ 1/1-1430 and in many major libraries in the UK and overseas.

The London Gazette published details of all Army Commissions, in both the Regular Army and in the Militia, so that the indexes may be used to trace such events for officers. Other ranks are less frequently mentioned, although full lists of Casualties were published in the Crimean War as well as lists of amounts due to the dependants of deceased soldiers following that conflict. During the siege at Sevastopol, for example, regular reports and nominal lists were published. The Second Supplement to the London Gazette, of Tuesday the 27th of November 1855, published on Thursday, November 29, 1855, reported the following among the wounded on the 15th November:

        Nominal Return of Non-Commissioned Officers and Privates
        WOUNDED on the 15th November 1855

        WOUNDED, by the explosion of magazines in camp
                (of French siege-train)

            19th Regiment of Foot

    1214   Corporal James Doorly, severely
    2987   Private Jeremiah O'Brien, severely
    2693   John Caldwell, contusion
    3319   Robert Sommerville, slightly
    3596   John Gearedd, slightly
    2485   John Sheehan, slightly
    2763   Edwin Herwood, severely
     887   William Beech, slightly

INDIAN ARMIES

Records of officers and men of the East India Company's armies, 1708-1861 and of the Indian Army, 1861-1947, are to be found in an extensive collection at the India Office Library and Records, 197 Blackfriars Road, London SE1, who have published a brief guide to biographical sources.[66] Separate sections give detailed summaries of material available on European Officers, Departmental and Warrant Officers, European NCOs and Privates, Medical and Veterinary Officers, Indian Officers and Other Ranks, and Bandsmen, for both periods mentioned above.

A further section of the guide lists some material, kept at the India Office Library, for officers and other ranks of British Army regiments stationed in India. For instance, lists of officers in British Army regiments are provided in the series Military Statements for Bengal 1785-1858, Madras 1794-1858 and Bombay 1791-1858. These are continued in the Bengal Army list 1819-89, the Madras Army list 1810-95, the Bombay Army list 1823-95 and the Indian Army list 1889-1947. Pension records are also available. For other ranks in the British Army regiments in India, the India Office Library has, for example, Chelsea Pension Accounts 1870-1942, and Lists of Chelsea Out-Pensions drawn in India 1873-1914.

Farrington[6,7] has produced a detailed listing of India Office military records, while Fitzhugh[68] has provided a general introduction to the subject of East India Company ancestry.

Most service records for officers and men of the British Army stationed in India will be found in the PRO (Kew) among the regimental and other documents already described in earlier sections. Additionally, at the PRO (Kew), there are Pension Returns (WO 22) for Bengal 1845-1880, Bombay 1855-1880 and Madras 1849-1869; Chelsea Registers (WO 23) for East India Company Pensioners 1814-1868; and, according to reference 76, details of men discharged between 1863 and 1875, in the musters of Victoria Hospital, Netley (WO 12/13017-13105), continued, between 1875 and 1889, in the musters of the discharge depot at Gosport (WO 16/2284, 2888-2915).

JOURNAL OF THE SOCIETY FOR ARMY HISTORICAL RESEARCH

The Society for Army Historical Research, founded in 1921, produces a quarterly journal which is the major publication dealing with historical matters relating to the British Army.[90] The first forty volumes (1921-1962) are indexed in an exemplary manner, first in a Subject Index, then in an Index to Regiments, Corps and Formations; finally there is a Concordance of Numbered and Named Regiments, which should settle most disputes about the precise dates and titles of the units of the British Army. An occasional series of Special

My Ancestor was in the British Army

Publications will cover a topic in more detail or fully reproduce an important source. For example, Special Publication Number 3 is a reprint of the earliest known printed Army List, of 1740.

Any genealogist with soldier ancestry can be strongly recommended to use this Journal. The first approach would be through the composite index for the first forty years, looking for the unit in which a soldier served. Much background material and research sources can be discovered, as well as a historical picture of service conditions. Volume 68 for 1990 contains, for example, an article on welfare measures for the sick and wounded of the nine year war in Ireland, 1593-1602.[92] A list of names is provided, with county and pension award, of about 250 disabled and aged soldiers who received relief. This volume also contains the concluding parts of an extensive article about a manuscript history of the 26th (or Cameronian) Regiment.[93] For the family historian, there are nominal lists of men for the period 1828 to 1840, when the regiment served in India; the lists relate to deaths and discharges of men, deaths of children, and to recipients of the regimental medal.

As a final example, there is a report of the first five years of the Army Records Society, which produces an annual volume of original material put into print for the first time. A leaflet about membership and availability of back volumes can be obtained from Dr Ian Beckett, Department of War Studies, RMA Sandhurst, Camberley, GU15 4PQ.

The Society of Army Historical Research can be reached via its Editor or its Secretary, c/o the National Army Museum, Royal Hospital Road, Chelsea, London SW3 4HT.

MISCELLANY

The variety of ancillary sources for army ancestry is clearly legion! Apart from the major collections of documents and original records that have been touched on in this booklet, there are numerous further records in county record offices and foreign archives, as well as in private papers and collections. Some bibliographies of document and printed material are available and are listed in the Further Reading lists in the Reference section (see page 88).

Family historians are themselves compiling many items of military interest. Several have been published by family history societies, either separately or in their journals. A selection of separately published lists is given at the end of the Reference section (see page 97). Fortunately, journal articles are being listed regularly in the Digest Section of the Family History News and Digest.[95] Prior to 1985, they are summarised in a sub-section "Institution and Service", from 1985 under "Armed Forces"; 150 articles during the last five years attest to the interest in this subject.

My Ancestor was in the British Army

WORLD WAR I RECORDS

This chapter is intended merely to provide a brief introduction to the subject of tracing army records for the World War I period. The 1914-1919 period is dealt with separately from the era preceding 1914 as soldiers' records have been retained by the Ministry of Defence. Three booklets about this conflict by Norman Holding have been published by the FFHS, giving a thorough review of a complicated subject.[37] [38] [39]

The records available to the public for tracing the career of a soldier during World War I are nowhere near as comprehensive as those for the period preceding 1914. The main reason for this is the requirement of confidentiality. It seems unlikely that the army personnel records for 1914-1919 will be transferred to the PRO (Kew) before 1993. Further, many of these records were destroyed or damaged by bombing during World War II. However, there are some clearly defined methods which can yield some specific information, and from this it may well prove possible to locate further background to a soldier's life in World War I, either from War Diaries at the PRO (Kew) or from regimental histories.

The Army Records Centre is discussed first in the following. If one wishes to trace the service of a soldier, one will need to approach this centre by correspondence. (Also, if one can consult the Medal Rolls (WO 329) at the PRO (Kew), this should trace most soldiers - see page 85.) However, if the soldier sought was killed during World War I, there are three sources from which one can obtain details. The most fruitful place to approach first is the Commonwealth War Graves Commission, who keep an overall index (see page 83 for details). Secondly, one can obtain information about a soldier's unit from the alphabetical indexes of deaths at St Catherine's House (see also page 23). Finally, the publication "Soldiers died in the Great War"[35] is discussed; to use this, however, one needs to have a good idea already of a soldier's regiment.

ARMY RECORDS CENTRE

The address of the Army Records Centre is Ministry of Defence, CS (Records) Z Section, Bourne Avenue, Hayes, Middlesex, UB3 1RF. Only written enquiries are accepted. It currently houses all personnel records of soldiers from 1914 onwards. (However, some material for officers commissioned early in World War I is now at the PRO, and the records of men discharged from the Army within the last 8 years are still at Army Record Centres.) It is difficult to obtain clear information about the precise records held; in the first case, there were upwards of 4 million persons involved, compared with probably fewer than half a million prior to 1914, so it can be seen that the quantity of records is vast. Further, records of other ranks have been either "weeded" or damaged by enemy action in World War II. (Fortunately, officers' records were merely weeded not bombed.) Charges for provision of information from records were introduced in 1988,[87] a search fee of £15 is required in advance, together with the usual proofs of kinship that are needed before releasing information from a personal record to a third party.

A request for information about an officer might elicit a response such as:

Lieutenant John Henry Heyman (Deceased)	
Born 29 June 1894	
Enlisted into Honourable Artillery Company	
(Infantry) embodied Territorial Force	
as No 2283	8 Sep 14
Discharged on Appointment to a Commission	19 Oct 15
Appointed to a Temporary Commission as	
2nd Lieutenant, Army Service Corps	20 Oct 15
Promoted Lieutenant	21 Jul 16
Attached 29th Siege Battery Royal Garrison	
Artillery	7 Mar 17
Died of wounds received in Action	18 Jul 17
Medals: 1914-15 Star, British War Medal, Victory Medal	

By contrast the records of other ranks were severely affected by the bombing in 1940; the extent of the losses has never been clearly publicised, but requests for information often result in a very brief statement, such as

Private Thomas Banks Watts
No 2389 Northumberland Fusiliers and A Cycle Coy
W 2/320870 Royal Engineers
Medals: 1915 Star, British War Medal, Victory Medal

COMMONWEALTH WAR GRAVES COMMISSION

"Some 1,700,000 Commonwealth servicemen and women died in the two world wars, 1914-1918 and 1939-1945, and to this day are remembered in the war cemeteries and Memorials to be found all over the world."

"In an overall index, held at the Commonwealth War Graves Commission Head Office in Maidenhead, the names of these war dead are recorded in alphabetical order by surname and include Number, Rank (Service), date of death and location of grave, or Memorial. These indexes are in coded form for convenience of official use and are not open to the general public. The Commission is always willing to supply information from these records of the location of a war grave, or Memorial of commemoration if there is no known grave. This information is supplied free of cost for relatives but, at the

discretion of the Commission, a charge of £1.00 per trace, whether
successful or not, may be made for research carried out on behalf of
authors, researchers, medal collectors, etc."

This extract from the information sheets of the Commission
indicates that a known grave can be readily located, provided of
course that one sends as much information as possible, e.g. full
names, rank, regiment or service, date of death and details of
next-of-kin or place of origin. The address to write to is: The
Enquiries Office, Commonwealth War Graves Commission, 2 Marlow Road,
Maidenhead, Berks SL6 7DX.

The Commission also operates an unofficial service, taking
photographs of particular graves or names on memorials but these
depend on visits by their supervisory staff to particular cemeteries.
A charge of a few pounds is made towards the costs involved. Their
publications include cemetery and memorial registers, listing the
dead of both World Wars and photocopies of individual pages can be
supplied. A typical example, taken from Index No B 16 to Dozinghem
Military Cemetery, Westvleteren, Belgium, reads

> HAYMAN, Lt. J. H. 29th Mechanical Transport
> Coy. Royal Army Service Corps, attd. 29th
> Siege Bty. Ammunition Col. "B" Siege Park,
> II. Corps. Died of wounds (gas) 18th July 1917.
> Age 23. Son of Henry and Elsie Hayman,
> of 48, Cheniston Gardens, Kensington, London.
> I. J. 1. (Plot, Row and Grave references.)

Copies of the individual cemetery registers, but not the composite
indexes, are held by many reference libraries and are being
reproduced on microfiche.[88]

INDEX TO WAR DEATHS AT ST CATHERINE'S HOUSE

The Index to War Deaths at St Catherine's House lists soldiers
alphabetically for the whole period 1914 to 1921; there are 9 volumes
for Other Ranks and a single volume for Officers. A typical entry in
the index would read:

> Watts, Percival J Pte 6071 RWKR 1915 Vol I 72 p 84

The corresponding death certificate confirmed that Private Percival
J Watts, Regimental Number 6071, had served in the 8th Battalion of
the Royal West Kent Regiment, that he had been born in England and
had been killed in action aged 19 in France on the 5th November 1915.
(There are corresponding indexes in the GROs at Edinburgh and Dublin
- see page 76.)

SOLDIERS DIED IN THE GREAT WAR

The publication "Soldiers died in the Great War 1914-1918"[35] is in 80 parts, arranged by Regiment or Corps, then by Battalion and then alphabetically; there is a single volume of "Officers died in the Great War 1914-1918".[36] The entry for Percival Watts was found in the 8th Battalion of the 53rd or Royal West Kent Regiment and reads:

> Watts, Percival John, b. Charlton, Kent, e. Woolwich,
> Kent (Blackheath, Kent), G/6071, Pte., k. in a.,
> F. & F., 5/11/15.

Places of birth, enlistment and residence (in brackets) are given, followed by number, rank; killed in action in "France and Flanders".

IMPERIAL WAR MUSEUM

The Imperial War Museum, Lambeth Road, London SE1 6HZ has major collections of material relating to the two World Wars (and also to conflicts since 1914 involving Great Britain or other members of the Commonwealth). These include manuscript papers, personal diaries, printed publications, photographs, maps, medals and uniforms. The Department of Printed Books maintains a large collection of regimental and other unit histories.

OTHER SOURCES FOR WORLD WAR I

There are of course numerous further sources for World War I and it is only possible to mention them briefly here.

The <u>Service Medal and Award Rolls, War of 1914-1918, (WO 329)</u> comprising 3273 volumes, were transferred from the Army Medal Office, Droitwich to the PRO (Kew) in 1987/8. They relate to the award to officers and other ranks of the Army and the Royal Flying Corps of the British War Medal, the Victory Medal, the 1914 Star, the 1914-1915 Star, the Territorial Force War Medal and the Silver War Badge. The registers in class WO 329 are accessed via an alphabetical card index, which is available to the public in microfiche form. As every British soldier who served in a theatre of war from 1914-1918 was entitled to the British War Medal, this index itself is invaluable; it gives details of the types of award made and the soldier's regiment, rank, and number. The registers often contain further information. (See also PRO Leaflet Number 101.[84])

At the PRO (Kew) the <u>War Diaries (WO 95)</u> of each unit, typically for battalions or larger, are available for search and can provide excellent background material, although they are unlikely to mention men by name. (See Holding.[37]) There are approximately 5500 boxes and files covering the period 1914 to 1922 in WO 95.

My Ancestor was in the British Army

The London Gazette may be searched for details of any awards or for details of promotions of officers. There are quarterly indexes which list awards under "State Intelligence"; names are given for recipients of the DCM, DSM, DSO, Foreign Orders, MC and MM. Those mentioned in despatches are then listed under "War Office". Military promotions are sub-divided into Commands and Staff, Regular Forces, Territorial Force, Volunteer Force, Overseas Contingents and Indian Army. PRO Leaflet No 105 gives further details on how to consult the London Gazette using references from the First World War service and medal award rolls (WO 329).[84]

The London Gazette itself (but not its indexes) contained alphabetical lists of "Soldiers' Balances Undisposed of", together with the sums due to those "supposing themselves entitled as Next of Kin". For instance, the issue for 30th November 1917 contained "List CCCCCIX of the names of deceased Soldiers whose Personal Estate is held for distribution ... Effects 1916-1917," as well as the "1st Re-publication of List CCCCXCIX " of the names of deceased Soldiers for 1915-1916. One wonders whether the relatives of Private R Clarke, Northamptonshire Regiment, ever claimed his £5/15/4, or if Cameron Highlander Corporal J Cameron's next of kin benefitted from his £30/4/4. (See also page 70 re Deceased Soldiers' Effects.)

Local newspapers should be searched for details of anyone receiving awards or mentioned in despatches; lists of wounded were often published while those killed were usually commemorated by a report and photograph.

There are numerous books, such as regimental histories, or regimental journals about World War I, but few record names of soldiers except in a Roll of Honour or a list of medal recipients. Bibliographies by Enser[42] and White[94] may be consulted.

Military photographs may be used to identify the unit in which an ancestor served, by examining cap badges, uniform, equipment or other insignia. A good introduction to this topic is to be found in David Barnes' contribution, "Identification and Dating of Military Uniforms", in "Family History in Focus".[85] A service identifying military photographs is offered by Mike Chappell.[95] Postmarks and Censor Stamps may also be used to identify the unit of the sender; a service is provided by Alistair Kennedy, joint author of "The Postal History of the British Army in WWI".[95]

During World War I the British Army executed 346 men, most for desertion but a few for cowardice or murder. Judge Anthony Babington is the first author to be granted access to the court martial records in the PRO and has written, in "For the Sake of Example",[40] the tragic stories of those subjected to the operation of military justice during wartime. The soldiers and officers concerned are not identified by Babington, but they are named in the book by Sykes and Putkowski.[41] The 72 volumes of registers for Field General Courts Martial and Military Courts (1909-1963) are in class WO 213 at the

PRO but remain closed for 100 years. As a tribute to these men an epitaph from the Bailleulmont Communal Cemetery in France may be quoted:[40]

> 10495 Private A Ingham, Manchester Regiment,
> 1st December 1916,
> Shot At Dawn, One of the First to Enlist,
> A Worthy Son of his Father.

A copy death certificate for Private Albert Ingham, age 24, is reproduced in Lyn Macdonald's "Voices and Images of the Great War".[43] The cause of death is given as "Shot by sentence of FGCM, for "Desertion"".

The British Red Cross, (Archives Section, Barnett Hill, Wonersh, Guildford, Surrey GU5 0RF), has good records of its own personnel and will search these for enquirers; a donation towards such work is welcomed. In this way we found that Henry Hayman (father of the Lt John Hayman, whose death in action was quoted above) had received the War Medal, for his work under the Joint War Committee of the British Red Cross and Order of St John during the First World War. The only records of British military personnel available date from the First World War and are contained in the British Red Cross and Order of St John Enquiry Lists for wounded and missing. The Archives Section has such lists only for February 1915; 18 May 1915; 26 June 1915; 17 July 1915; 24 July 1915; 31 July 1915; 7 August 1915; 4 September 1915; 18 September 1915; 1 September 1916; 15 September 1916. The regiment must be known in order to search these lists. A further Enquiry List, No 14, 1917, containing all enquiries up to and including 20 July 1917, is available and has recently been published by Sunset Militaria.

The International Committee of the Red Cross, (Central Tracing Agency, Geneva) holds records for British prisoners of war for both World Wars. Enquiries may be directed through the British Red Cross. Information is normally passed only to next of kin and enquiries of a compassionate nature take priority over those researching their family history. A typical reply gave details of 29074 Private William Hughes, born at Birkdale on 5 October 1896; his unit was the 13th King's (Liverpool Regiment), he was captured on 28 March 1918, interned in Langensalze camp at 10 August 1918 and had received wounds in the right arm and shoulder.

The Western Front Association (Frank E Smith, 6 Edgehill Road, Doncaster, South Yorks DN2 5QT) is making an index of wounded other ranks, using official lists in local newspapers. (Send a SSAE.) Membership is open to all interested in the 1914-1918 period, with particular reference to France and Flanders.

REFERENCES and BIBLIOGRAPHY

INTRODUCTION and GENERAL - ARMY

1 Hamilton-Edwards, Gerald, *In search of army ancestry*, Phillimore, 1977.

2 Palmer, Roy, *The rambling soldier - life in the lower ranks, 1750-1900, through soldiers' songs and writings*, Penguin/Peacock Books, 1977 and 1986.

3 Neuburg, Victor, *Gone for a soldier - a history of life in the British ranks from 1642*, Cassell, 1989.

4 Brereton, J.M., *A guide to the regiments and corps of the British army on the regular establishment*, Bodley Head, 1985.

5 Brereton, J.M., *The British soldier - a social history from 1661 to the present day*, Bodley Head, 1986.

6 Fortescue, Sir John William, *A history of the British army*, Macmillan, 13 volumes, 1899-1930.

<u>Further Reading - Army</u>

Bruce, Anthony (ed), *A bibliography of British military history from the Roman invasion to the Restoration*, K.G.Saur, Munich, 1981.

Hallows, Ian S., *Regiments and Corps of the British army*, Arms and Armour Press, London, 1991. (Includes details of regimental journals, histories, museums and associations.)

Higham, Robin (ed), *A guide to the sources of British military history*, Routledge and Kegan Paul, 1972.

Kitzmuller II, John M., *In search of the "forlorn hope": a comprehensive guide to locating British regiments and their records (1640-WWI)*, Manuscript Publishing Foundation, Salt Lake City, 1988.

British Library Catalogue, *BLC to 1975*, Volumes 96 and 97, pages 891 to 1092, cover publications about the army; army lists, p 931 et seq.

OFFICERS (prior to 1914)

7 Dalton, Charles, *English army lists and commission registers, 1661-1714*, Eyre & Spottiswoode, 6 volumes, 1892-1904.

8 Dalton, Charles, *The Blenheim roll, 1704*, Eyre & Spottiswoode, 1899. (This is also included in Volume V of the previous reference).

9   Dalton, Charles, *George I's Army, 1714-1727*, Eyre & Spottiswoode, 2 volumes, 1910.

10 *Army list* - official annual publication since 1754.

11 Hart, H.G., *Army list* - published annually, 1840-1915.

12 Peterkin A., Johnston W. & Drew R., *Commissioned officers in the medical services of the British army, 1660-1960*, Wellcome Historical Medical Library, 1968.

13 Askwith W.H., *List of officers of the Royal Regiment of Artillery, 1716-1899*, 1900.

14 Askwith W.H. & Morgan F.C., *List of officers of the Royal Regiment of Artillery, Volume II, 1862-1914*, Sheffield, 1914.

15 Conolly T.W.J. & Edwards R.F., *Roll of Officers of the Royal Engineers, 1660-1898*, Chatham, 1898.

16 Bruce, Anthony, *The purchase system in the British army, 1660-1871*, Royal Historical Society, 1980.

17 *House of Commons Journals* (see appendix 2, Army Estimates), Vol 68 (1812-3) pp 716-9, 69 (1813-4) 560-5, 70 (1814-6) 539-548, 71 (1816-7) 587-9, 72 (1817) 528-542, 73 (1818) 469-484, 74 (1818-9) 682, 75 (1819-20) 526.

18 Dalton, Charles, *Waterloo roll call*, William Clowes & Son, London, 1890; Eyre & Spottiswoode, London, 2nd edn, 1904; 2nd edn reprinted, Arms & Armour Press, London, 1971.
(NB Lists all regiments, and all officers, at Waterloo.)

Further Reading - Officers (prior to 1914)

Reid, Stuart, *Officers and regiments of the royalist army, being a revised list of indigent officers, 1663*, in five volumes, Partisan Press, 26 Cliffsea Grove, Leigh-on-Sea, Essex SS9 1NQ, 1985?.

Dalton, Charles, *Irish army lists, 1661-1685*, London, 1907.

Dalton, Charles, *The Scots army, 1661-1688*, Eyre & Spottiswoode, London and William Brown, Edinburgh, 1909; reprint Greenhill Books, 1989.

OTHER RANKS (prior to 1914)

19 Watts, Christopher T. and Michael J., *In search of a soldier ancestor*, Genealogists' Magazine, 19 (4) 125-128, 1977.

20 Williams, Robert G. and Llewellyn, Howard (transcribed by), *Persons in 1881 stationed at Maindy barracks, St. John's Parish, Cardiff*, Glamorgan FHS Journal No 8, December 1985.

21 Kenzie, K., (transcribed by), *Bradford Moor barracks census 1851*, Bradford FHS Newsletter No 20, September 1990.

22 Oliver, Rosemary M., *War Office district pension returns*, Genealogists' Magazine, 21 (6) 196-199, 1984.

23 Pike, Sheila, *Could your ancestor be here?*, Devon Family Historian, July 1984, 10-14.

24 Barlow, Angela, *War Office musters*, Journal of the Manchester and Lancashire FHS, 26 (2), April 1990.

PARTICULAR CAMPAIGNS, BATTLES and ACTIONS

25 Glover, Michael, *Wellington's army in the Peninsula, 1808-1814*, David and Charles, 1977.

26 Dwelly, E., *Muster roll of British NCOs and men at the battle of Waterloo: Part I Cavalry*, privately published, Fleet, Hants, 1934.

Further Reading - Particular Campaigns, Battles and Actions

Lummis, William M. and Wynn, Kenneth G., *Honour the Light Brigade*, J.B. Hayward & Son, London, 1973. (Ts index by H.N. Peyton at SoG.)

Cook, F. & A., *Casualty roll for the Crimea, 1854-55*, J.B. Hayward & Son, London, 1976.

Hibbard, M.G., *List of casualties in South African Field Force, 11 Oct 1899 to 31 May 1902*, 1972. (Facsimile of WO 108/338.)

MILITIA AND AUXILIARY FORCES

27 Gibson, Jeremy and Dell, Alan, *Tudor and Stuart muster rolls, a directory of holdings in the British Isles*, Federation of Family History Societies, 1989.

28 Gibson, Jeremy and Medlycott, Mervyn, *Militia lists and musters, 1757-1876, a directory of holdings in the British Isles*, Federation of Family History Societies, 1989.

29 Medlycott, Sir Mervyn, *Some Georgian "Censuses" - the Militia and "Defence" Lists*, Genealogists' Magazine, 23 (2), 55-59, 1989.

30 Beckett, I.F.W., *The amateur military tradition*, Manchester University Press, 1991.

31 Arnison, Janet, *A roll of the Westmorland Militia (from D/LONS/L 13/6/26 at Cumbria RO)*, Cumbria FHS Newsletter Number 41, 1986.

32 *The Craven muster roll 1803, North Yorkshire County Record Office Publication Number 9*, North Yorkshire County Council, 1976.

33 Lawes, Edward, *Militia records*, Hampshire Family Historian, 8 (4), February 1982.

34 Cunningham, Hugh, *The volunteer force - a social and political history, 1859-1908*, Croom Helm, London, 1975.

WORLD WAR I (see also reference 88)

35 *Soldiers died in the Great War 1914-1919 (80 parts)*, Imperial War Museum, HMSO, 1921-2.

36 *Officers died in the Great War 1914-1919*, HMSO, 1919. (Also reprints by Samson, 1975 & 1979; new enlarged edition by J.B. Hayward, Polstead, Suffolk, 1988; latter includes three new appendices, listing Deceased Regular Army Officers, Deceased Territorial Force Army Officers and Deceased European Officers of the Indian Army.)

37 Holding, Norman H., *World War I army ancestry*, Federation of Family History Societies (FFHS), 2nd edition 1991.

38 Holding, Norman H., *The location of British army records: A national directory of World War I sources*, FFHS, 3rd edn 1991.

39 Holding, Norman H., *More sources of World War I army ancestry*, FFHS, 2nd edition 1991.

40 Babington, Anthony, *For the sake of example, capital courts martial, 1914-1920*, Secker and Warburg, 1983; Paladin 1985.

41 Sykes, Julian & Putkowski, Julian, *Shot at dawn*, Wharncliffe Publishing, Barnsley, 1989.

42 Enser, A.G.S., *A subject bibliography of the First World War - books in English, 1914-1978*, Deutsch, London, 1979.

43 Macdonald, Lyn, *1914-1918, Voices and images of the Great War*, Michael Joseph 1988, Penguin 1991.

Further Reading - World War I

Carmichael, Jane (Keeper of Department of Photographs, Imperial War Museum), *First World War photographers*, Routledge, 1989.

Gould, Robert W., *Locations of British cavalry, infantry and machine gun units, 1914-1924*, Heraldene Ltd, 1977.

Laffin, John, *World War I in postcards*, Alan Sutton Publishing Ltd.,
Brunswick Road, Gloucester, 1989.

Pals Series: (includes nominal rolls and medal lists).
Liverpool Pals (17th-20th Bns, The Kings), Graham Maddocks, 1991.
Leeds Pals (15th Bn, Prince of Wales Own), Laurie Milner, 1991.
Accrington Pals (11th East Lancs), William Turner, 1987.
Sheffield City (12th York & Lancaster), Oldfield & Gibson, 1988.
Barnsley Pals (13th-14th York & Lancaster), Jon Cooksey, 1986.
Leo Cooper Pen & Sword Books, 47 Church St, Barnsley, S70 2BR.

HONOURS, MEDALS and MUSEUMS

44 Norman, C.B., *Battle honours of the British army, 1662-1901*,
Murray, 1911. (David and Charles Reprints, 1971.)

45 Joslin, E.C., *Spink's catalogue of British and associated orders,
decorations and medals with valuations*, Webb and Bower, 1983.

46 Leslie N.B., *Battle honours of the British and Indian armies,
1695-1914*, Leo Cooper, 1970.

47 Foster, Col. K.O.N., *The Military General Service Medal,
1793-1814*, Berlin/London, 1947.

48 Abbott, P.E., *Recipients of the Distinguished Conduct Medal,
1855-1909*, J.B. Hayward & Son, 1975.

49 Gould, R.W. (compiler of army section), *The Army of India Medal
Roll, 1799-1826*, from WO 100/13, J.B. Hayward & Son, 1974.

50 *South Africa, 1899-1902. Officers and men of the army and navy
mentioned in despatches*, London, 1902, reprinted 1971.

51 Creagh, Sir O'Moore and Humphris, E.M., *The Victoria Cross
(1856-1920) and the Distinguished Service Order (1886-1923)*, 3
volumes, (I VC, II & III DSO), London, 1924. (Hayward reprint.)

52 Skingley, Andrew J., *Medal hunting*, Essex Family Historian,
Spring 1984, 32, 24-26.

53 Wise, Terence, *A guide to military museums*, Athena Books,
20 St Mary's Rd, Doncaster DN1 2NP, 5th edn 1986.

Further Reading - Honours, Medals and Museums

Purves, Alec A., *Collecting medals and decorations*, Seaby, London,
3rd edition 1978.

Alcock, Sheila (ed), *Museums and art galleries in Great Britain
and Ireland*, British Leisure Publications, annual.

My Ancestor was in the British Army

The Register of the Victoria Cross, This England Books, Alma House, Rodney Road, Cheltenham, 1981 and 1988.

BRITISH SOLDIERS ABROAD

Australia
54 Peake, Andrew G., *Army pension records in Australia*, Genealogists' Magazine, 21 (10) 368, 1985.

55 Fitzmaurice, Yvonne, *Army deserters from H.M. Service: Volume 1, 1853-1858; Volume 2 (in Australia and New Zealand), 1853-1870;* published by author, 23 Fuller St, Mitcham, Victoria 3132, 1988.

56 Sexton, Rae, *The deserters - a complete record of military and naval deserters in Australia and New Zealand, 1800-65*, Australasian Maritime Historical Society, Box 33, Magill S. A. 5072, 1985.

57 Montague, R.H., *How to trace your military ancestors in Australia and New Zealand*, Hale and Iremonger, GPO Box 2552, Sydney, NSW, 1989.

58 *Australian Joint Copying Project Handbook: Part 1, General Introduction*, 1985; *Part 4, War Office*, 1986.

59 Bradley, Joyce et al, *Roll Call! - a guide to genealogical sources in the Australian War Memorial*, Australian War Memorial, Canberra, ACT 2601, 1986.

60 *Relations in records. A guide to family history sources in the Australian Archives.* Australian Government Publishing Service, Canberra, 1988.

Canada
61 *Checklist of parish registers*, Manuscript Division, Public Archives of Canada, 395 Wellington Street, Ottawa, Ontario, K1A 0N3, 3rd edn, 1981. (Holy Trinity, Quebec, Anglican Registers, 1768-1800, on films C-2897 and C-2898. Quebec Garrison Protestant Chaplaincy registers, 1797-1800, 1817-1826, on films C-2898 and C-2899.)

62 *Tracing your ancestors in Canada* (see section on Military and Naval Records), Public Archives of Canada, as above, 8th edn, 1984. (Material about Royal Warwickshire Regiment, 6th Regiment of Foot, is in RG 8, Volumes 829-831, on films C-3266 and C-3267.)

63 *General inventory manuscripts, Vol 2 (MG11 - MG16), Vol 3 (MG17 - MG21), Vol 4 (MG22 - MG25)*, Public Archives of Canada, from 1972.

64 Private communication from Archives Nationales du Quebec, 1210, avenue du Seminaire, Case postale 10450, Sainte-Foy (Quebec) G1V 4N1. (Garrison of Quebec Anglican Church registers, 1797-1871, available on films M 138/22 to 24; outside Canada, purchase from "Federation des associations de familles-souches" at same address. SoG has microfilm copies of Quebec Anglican Church registers for 1797-1815.)

Gibraltar
65 Burness, Lawrence R., *Genealogical research in Gibraltar*, Genealogists' Magazine, 21 (1) 21-2, 1983.

India
66 Baxter, I.A., *India Office library and records: a brief guide to biographical sources*, 1959.

67 Farrington, Anthony, *Guide to the records of the India Office military department*, IOLR Guide to Archives 2, London, 1982.

68 Fitzhugh, T.V.H., *East India Company ancestry*, Genealogists' Magazine, 21 (5) 150-4, 1984.

New Zealand (see also under Australia)
69 Hughes, Hugh and Lyn, *Discharged in New Zealand - soldiers of the Imperial foot regiments who took their discharge in New Zealand, 1840-1870*, NZ Society of Genealogists, Box 8795, Auckland; 1988.

70 Kendall, Shirley E., *The Pensioner Gazette*, PO Box 139, Penshurst NSW 2222, 1987 onwards.

71 *Family history at National Archives*, Allen & Unwin and National Archives (NZ), 1990.

United States of America
72 Eakle, Arlene and Cerny, Johni, *The source - a guidebook of American genealogy*, Ancestry Publishing Company, Salt Lake City, Utah, 1984. (See Chapter 8, Military Records.)

73 *Guide to genealogical research in the National Archives*, National Archives Guide, PO Box 37066, Washington DC 20013; 1988.

General Overseas
74 Yeo, Geoffrey, *The British overseas: a guide to records of their births, baptisms, marriages, deaths and burials available in the United Kingdom*, Guildhall Library, London, 2nd edn 1988.

75 *Abstract of arrangements respecting registration of births, marriages and deaths in the United Kingdom and the other countries of the British Commonwealth and in the Irish Republic*, HMSO, 1952.

Further Reading - British Soldiers Abroad

Mason, Philip, *A matter of honour*, 1974, Papermac 1986. (History of Indian Army.)

PUBLIC RECORD OFFICE

76 *Records of officers and soldiers who have served in the British army*, Public Record Office, 20pp booklet, 1984.

77 *List of War Office records preserved in the PRO, Volume I,* PRO Lists and Indexes Number XXVIII, 1908.

78 *War Office and other military records preserved in the PRO,* PRO Lists and Indexes Number LIII, 1931. (An alphabetical guide.)

79 *List of War Office records,* PRO Lists and Indexes, Supplementary Series, Vol. VIII: 1, Kraus Reprints, 1968.

80 *List of War Office records,* PRO Lists and Indexes, Supplementary Series, Vol. VIII: 2, Kraus Reprints, 1968.

81 *Soldiers' Documents, 1760-1913, (WO 97),* List and Index Society, Volume 201, 1983.

82 *Muster Books and Pay Lists, General Series, 1760-1877, (WO 12/ 1-13305),* List and Index Society, Volume 210, 1984. (N.B. This volume lists infantry, cavalry and many other corps, not just cavalry, as incorrectly stated on the title page.)

83 Wynne-Davies, Mrs Lesley, *Volunteers' projects - WO 97,* Prophile, (Journal of the Friends of the Public Record Office), Volume 2, Number 1, Spring 1991.

84 PRO Information Leaflets

Means of reference at Kew, Number 36.
Operational records of the British army in the War of 1914 to 1919, Number 6.
Militia muster rolls, 1522-1640. Number 46.
Operational records of the British army, 1660-1914, Number 61.
Records of the Board of Ordnance, Number 67.
Prisoners of war 1660-1919: documents in the PRO, Number 72.
Records of courts martial: army, Number 84.
Service medal and award rolls: War of 1914-1918, WO 329, Number 101.
First World War: indexes to medal entitlement, Number 105.
Records of medals, Number 108.
Military maps of World War I, Number 115.

PRO - General Bibliography

Cox, Jane and Padfield, Timothy, *Tracing your ancestors in the Public Record Office,* 4th edn (by Bevan, A. and Duncan, A.) 1990.

Guide to the contents of the Public Record Office, Volume I, legal records etc, HMSO, 1963.

Guide to the contents of the Public Record Office, Volume II, state papers and departmental records, HMSO, 1963.

Guide to the contents of the Public Record Office, Volume III, documents transferred 1960-1966, HMSO, 1968.

Public Record Office guide, Parts II and III, published regularly on microfiche.

GENERAL GENEALOGICAL WORKS (references only)

85 Steel, Don and Taylor, Lawrence (editors), *Family history in focus*, Lutterworth Press, 1984.

86 Hood, Christine (ed), *Norwich Archdeaconry marriage licence bonds, 1813-1837*, Norfolk Genealogy Vol 23, Norfolk and Norwich Genealogical Society, 1991.

87 *Military service records search fees*, Genealogists' Magazine, 22 (10), 371, 1988.

88 *Catalogue of British official publications not published by HMSO*, annual publication, Chadwyck Healey. For cemetery indexes available on microfiche, see under Commonwealth War Graves Commission; eg for 1990, Nos 2367 to 2420.

89 Gorry, Paul, *The unusual problems of Irish research*, Family Tree Magazine, Vol 3 No 3 11-12, Jan 1987.

JOURNALS, SOCIETY and OCCASIONAL PUBLICATIONS

90 *Journal of the Society for Army Historical Research (JSAHR)*, published quarterly, 1921-date, c/o National Army Museum, Royal Hospital Road, Chelsea, London SW3 4HT.

91 Goulden, R.J., *Deserter bounty certificates*, JSAHR 50(1972), 161-168. (At PRO in E 182, Exchequer, KR, Receivers' Accounts of Land and Assessed Taxes, Subsidiary Documents.)

92 McGurk, J.J.N., *Casualties and welfare measures for the sick and wounded of the Nine Year War in Ireland, 1593-1602*, JSAHR 68(1990), 22-35, 188-204.

93 Wood, Stephen (Keeper, Scottish United Services Museum), *Thomas Carter and a manuscript history of the 26th (or Cameronian) regiment*, JSAHR 65(1987) 23-45, 148-170; 67(1989), 184-194; 68(1990), 51-55, 120-127.

94 White, Arthur S., *A bibliography of regimental histories of the British army*, JSAHR, 1965.

95 *Family History News and Digest (FHND)*, twice-yearly journal of the Federation of Family History Societies (FFHS), c/o Benson Room, Birmingham and Midland Institute, Margaret Street, Birmingham B3 3BS.

Post marks and censor stamps, Alistair Kennedy, 4 High St, Puckeridge, Ware, Herts, FHND 4 No 1 p 48, Spring 1983.

Military photographs, Mike Chappell, 1A High St, Hatherleigh, Devon EX20 3JH, FHND 4 No 1 p 48 and FHND 6 No 2, Sept 1987.

Unissued military medals, Capt (retd) Erik Gray, FHND 8 No 1, Apr 1991.

96 Gibson, J.S.W., *Marriage, census and other indexes for family historians*, FFHS, 4th edn, 1991.

97 Gibson, J.S.W., *Unpublished personal name indexes in record offices and libraries*, FFHS, 2nd edn 1985 (updated to 1988).

Many lists of regional interest have been compiled, and several published by family history societies separately or in their journals. A selection is given here:

98 *Channel Islands* Family History Journal, 34, Spring 1987, includes stray marriages at St Helier, Jersey, 1815-1824.

99 Index of stray registrations, Vol 2, extracted from *Cornwall* parish registers, H.N. Peyton, Ts, 1959. (Mainly military - only at SoG.)

100 *Leicestershire* Military Index, Vol 1, Royal Marines enlisted 1755-1820, born in Leicestershire & Rutland, Sue Brown, Leicester FHS, 1984?

101 *Leicestershire* Military Index, Vol 2, Chelsea Pensioners, applications for outpensions 1814-1831, from men born in Leicestershire and Rutland, (WO 116/17-40), Sue Brown, Leicester FHS, 1986.

102 *Leicestershire* Military Index, Vol 3, Chelsea Pensioners, applications for outpensions 1832-1855, from men born in Leicestershire and Rutland, (WO 116/41-59 and 125-129), Sue Brown, Leicester FHS, 1991?

103 *Lincolnshire* Veterans of the 5th Foot, Chelsea Out-Pensioners 1806-1838, from WO 120/23, J Robert Williams, Lincs FHS Journal Vol 2 No 4, July 1983.

104 *Sussex* Military Marriages, 1750-1812, Michael Burchall, Sussex Family History Group, 2/33 Sussex Square, Brighton BN2 5AB.

REFERENCES and BIBLIOGRAPHY

APPENDIX 1

CAMPAIGNS AND MEDALS — 1660-1902

(compiled from Norman[44] and PRO List and Index[79])

YEARS	CAMPAIGN/REGION	HONOURS
1662-1783	Mediterranean	Tangier (1662-1680), Gibraltar (1704 and 1779-1783)
1695-1709	Northern Europe	Namur (1695), Blenheim (1704), Ramillies (1706), Oudenarde (1708), Malplaquet (1709)
1743-1762	Northern Europe	Dettingen (1743), Minden (1759), Emsdorff (1760), Warburg (1760), Wilhelmstahl (1762)
1751-1764	India	Arcot (1751), Plassey (1757), Condore (1758), Masulipatam (1759), Badara (1759), Wandewash (1760), Buxar (1764)
1758-1759	North America	Louisburg (1758), Quebec (1759)
1759-1762	West Indies	Guadeloupe (1759), Martinique (1762), Havana (1762)
1774-1799	India	Rohilcund (1774), Guzerat (1778-1782), Sholingur (1781) Mangalore (1783), Nundy Droog (1791), Rohilcund (1794), Seedaseer (1799), Seringapatam (1799)
1778-1810	West Indies	St. Lucia (1778, 1796, 1803), Martinique (1794, 1809), Surinam (1804), Dominica (1805), Guadeloupe (1810)
1793-1799	Flanders	Lincelles (1793), Nieuport (1793), Villers-en-Couche, Beaumont, Willems, Tournay (1794), Egmont-op-Zee (1799)

For Campaign Medals - the list below continues to give all actions for which regimental, but not necessarily individual, honours were awarded   - see WO 100 /

YEARS	CAMPAIGN/REGION	HONOURS	
1793-1814	Peninsula	Rolica, Vimiera, Sahagun (1808), Corunna, Douro, Talavera (1809), Busaco (1810), Barrosa, Fuentes d'Onor, Albuera, Almaraz, Arroyos dos Molinos, Tarifa (1811) Ciudad Rodrigo, Badajoz, Salamanca (1812), Vittoria, Pyrenees, San Sebastian, Nivelle, Nive (1813), Orthes, Toulouse (1814)	1- 11 & 16
1801-1802	Egypt and Sudan	Mandora, Marabout (1801), Egypt (1802)	12
1803-1809	India	Ally Ghur (1803), Delhi (1803-4), Assaye (1803), Laswarree (1803), Deig (1803-4), Cochin (1809)	13
1806	Naples	Maida (1806)	
1806	South Africa	Cape of Good Hope (1806)	
1807	South America	Montevideo (1807)	
1812-1814	North America	Detroit (1812), Miami, Chateaugay, Chrystler's Farm (1813), Niagara, Bladensburg (1814)	

YEARS	CAMPAIGN/REGION	HONOURS	WO 100/
1815	Belgium	Ligny, Quatre Bras (16 June), Waterloo (18 June)	14- 15
1817-1826	India	Kirkee, Poona, Seetabuldee, Nagpoor,	13
		Maheidpoor (1817), Corygaum (1818),	
		Nowah (1819), Bhurtpore (1826)	
1809-1857	Minor Eastern	Arabia - Beni Boo Alli (1809 & 1821),	
	Campaigns	Bourbon (1810), Java (1811), Persian Gulf (1819),	
		Aden (1839), Persia (1856-57),	
		Bushire, Reshire (1856), Koosh-ab (1857)	
1824-1825	Burma	Ava, Kemmendine (1824), Arracan (1825)	
1835-1853	South Africa	South Africa (1835, 1846-47, 1851-53)	17
1839-1842	Afghanistan	Ghuznee, Khelat (1839), Kahun (1840),	20
		Jellalabad (1841-2), Kelat-i-Ghilzie,	
		Candahar, Ghuznee, Cabul (1842)	
1840-1842	China	Canton, Chusan (1841)	
1843	India	Scinde - Meeanee, Hyderabad	
		Gwalior - Maharajore, Punniar	
1845-1846	India (Sutlej)	Moodkee, Ferozeshah (1845), Aliwal,	
		Sobraon (1846)	
1848-1849	India (Punjab)	Chillianwallah, Mooltan, Goojerat (1849)	13
1846-1866	New Zealand	New Zealand (1846-7, 1860-1, 1863-6)	18
1852-1853	Burma	Pegu	
1854-1855	Crimea	Alma, Balaclava, Inkerman (1854),	22- 34
		Sevastopol (1854-55)	
1857-1859	Indian Mutiny	Delhi, Lucknow (1857), Central India (1857-58)	35- 39
1857-1860	China	Fatshan, Canton (1857), Taku Forts (1858	40- 41
		& 1860), Pekin (1860)	
1867-1868	Abyssinia		43
1873-1874	Ashanti	Ashanti, Coomassie	44
1877-1879	South Africa	Zulu War - Isandhlwana, Rorke's Drift	46- 50
1878-1880	Afghanistan	Ali Musjid (1878), Peiwar Kotal, Charasia, Kabul	51- 53
		(1879), Ahmed Khel, Maiwand, Kandahar (1880)	
1882-1884	Egypt	Tel-el-Kebir (1882), El-Teb, Tamaai (1884)	55- 61
1884-1889	Sudan	The Nile (1884-5), Abu Klea, Kirbekan,	62- 68
		Suakin, Tofrek (1885)	
1885-1887	Burma	Burma	69- 70
1895-1902	India	Chitral (1895), Malakand, Samana (1897),	73- 75
	(NW Frontier)	Tirah (1897-8), Waziristan (1901-2)	84- 89
1896-1898	Egypt and Sudan	Hafir (1896), Atbara (1898), Khartoum	80- 83
		incl Omdurman (1898)	
1892-1900	African	West Africa (1892-4), Ashanti (1896),	76- 79
	Campaigns	East and Central Africa / Uganda (1897-9)	
		Ashanti / Kumassi (1900)	
1900	China	Pekin (1900)	94- 99
1899-1902	South Africa	Talana, Elandslaagte, Belmont, Modder River	112-371
	(Boer War)	(1899), Tugela Heights, Kimberley, Ladysmith,	
		Paardeburg, Driefontein, Wepener, Johannesburg,	
		Laing's Nek, Diamond Hill, Witterburgen, Mafeking,	
		Belfast (1900)	

APPENDIX 2 — REGIMENTAL RECORDS
(Notes and abbreviations on page 120)

CAVALRY with best known pre-1914 titles and dates of original formation	MUSTER BOOKS & PAY LISTS Years	WO12/	REGIMENTAL REGISTERS Marriages Birth/Bapt Years	Years
Household Cavalry				
1st Life Guards	1660 1759-1877	1- 32	1870-1921	1870-1921
2nd Life Guards	1660 1788-1877	33- 51	1870-1921	1870-1921
Royal Horse Guards - The Blues	1660 1759-1877	52- 80		
Cavalry of the Line			(1794-1848	1800-1848)
1st (King's) Dragoon Guards	1685 1760-1878	81- 137	(1885-1908	1885-1908)
2nd Dragoon Guards (Queen's Bays)	1685 1760-1878	138- 189		
3rd (Prince of Wales's) Dr Gds	1685 1760-1878	190- 240	For 2nd to 7th	
4th (Royal Irish) Dr Gds	1685 1774-1878	241- 292	Dragoon Guards	
5th (Princess Charlotte of Wales's)			there are some	
Dragoon Guards	1685 1772-1878	293- 347	Registers for	
6th Dragoon Guards (Carabiniers)	1685 1760-1878	348- 399	ca 1877-1908	
7th (Princess Royal's) Dr Gds	1688 1760-1878	400- 452		
1st (Royal) Dragoons	1661 1760-1878	453- 507		
2nd Dragoons (Royal Scots Greys)	1668 1760-1878	508- 562	For Dragoons,	
3rd (King's Own) Hussars	1685 1760-1877	563- 620	Hussars and	
4th (Queen's Own) Hussars	1685 1760-1877	621- 681	Lancers there	
5th (Royal Irish) Lancers	1689/1858 1770-1799	682- 684	are some	
	1858-1878	685- 703	Registers for	
6th (Inniskilling) Dragoons	1689 1760-1878	704- 755	ca 1840-1908	
7th (Queen's Own) Hussars	1690 1760-1878	756- 810		
8th (King's Royal Irish) Hussars	1693 1771-1878	811- 868		
9th (Queen's Royal) Lancers	1715 1774-1877	869- 921		
10th (Prince of Wales's Own				
Royal) Hussars	1715 1760-1877	922- 975		
11th (Prince Albert's Own) Hussars	1715 1760-1877	976-1036		
12th (Prince of Wales's Ryl) L'crs	1715 1774-1876	1037-1083		
13th Hussars	1715 1771-1877	1084-1140		
14th (King's) Hussars	1715 1772-1877	1141-1191		
15th (The King's) Hussars	1746/1759 1760-1877	1192-1244		
16th (The Queen's) Lancers	1759 1760-1878	1245-1305		
17th (Duke of Cambridge's O) L'crs	1759 1771-1878	1306-1362		
18th (Queen Mary's Own) H'rs	1759/1858 1760-1878	1363-1398	(gap from 1822-1857)	
19th (Q Alexandra's O R) H'rs	1759/1858 1779-1878	1399-1417	(gap from 1822-1861)	
20th Hussars	1759/1858 1779-1878	1418-1440	(gap from 1819-1861)	
21st (Emp's of India's) L'crs	1760/1858 1779-1878	1441-1466	(gap from 1821-1862)	
22nd Dragoons	1779/1794/1802 1779-1820	1467-1478		
23rd Dragoons/Lancers	1781/1794/1803 1795-1817	1479-1488		
24th Dragoons	1794/1803 1794-1819	1489-1500		
25th Dragoons	1794/1803 1794-1819	1501-1511		
26th Dragoons	1795 1795-1802	1512-1514		
27th Dragoons	1795 1795-1802	1515		
28th Dragoons	1795 1795-1802	1516-1518		
29th Dragoons	1795 1795-1808	1519-1520	(gap from 1805-1806)	
30th-33rd Dragoons	1794 1795-1796	1521		

DESCRIPTION AND SUCCESSION BOOKS Years WO25/	SERVICE RETURNS No 1 WO25/	MMG's Cas. Index WO25/	INDEX TO CASUALTY RETURNS WO25/	CASUALTY RETURNS Years WO25/	SOLDIERS' DOCUMENTS 1760-1854 WO97/	1855-1872 WO97/
	871			1823-1857 1363-1365	1- 11	1272-1274
	872			1832-1851 1366-1368	1- 11	1272-1274
	873		2411	1810-1851 1359-1362	1- 11	1272-1274
1801-1874 266-268	877	1196	2412-3	1809-1830 1369-1372	All Cavalry of the	
	878	1196	2414-5	1809-1831 1373-1375	Line arranged	
	879	1197	2416-7	1809-1830 1376-1378	alphabetically in	
	880	1197	2418-9	1809-1831 1379-1381		
	881	1198	2420-1	1809-1830 1382-1384	WO97/	WO97/
					12- 149	1275-1305
	882	1198	2422-3	1810-1830 1385-1388		
1791-1829 269-272	883	1199	2424-5	1809-1830 1389-1391		
	884	1200	2426-7	1809-1830 1392-1394		
1813-1875 273-274	885	1200	2428-9	1809-1830 1395-1397		
1772-1833 275-277	886	1201	2430-1	1809-1852 1398-1404		
	887	1201	2432-3	1809-1842 1405-1412		
		1202				
	888	1202	2434-5	1809-1830 1413-1415		
	889	1203	2436-7	1809-1831 1416-1418		
	890	1203	2438-9	1809-1830 1419-1422		
	891	1204	2440-1	1809-1830 1423-1425		
	892	1204	2442-3	1809-1855 1426-1431		
1813-1878 278	893	1205	2444-5	1809-1837 1432-1436		
	894	1205	2446-7	1809-1830 1437-1441		
	895	1206	2448-9	1809-1830 1442-1445		
	896	1206	2450-1	1809-1830 1446-1448		
	897	1207	2452-3	1809-1854 1449-1453		
	898	1207	2454-5	1809-1846 1454-1458		
	899	1208	2456-7	1810-1830 1459-1462		
1783-1821 279-282	900	1208	2458-9	1809-1821 1463-1464		
1807-1821 283	901	1209	2460-1	1809-1821 1465-1466		
1795-1818 284-288	902	1209	2462-3	1809-1818 1467-1469		
1806-1820 289-292	903	1210	2464-5	1809-1830 1470-1471		
1796-1820 293-298	904	1210	2466-7	1810-1820 1472-1474		
1813-1817 299	905		2468	1809-1817 1475		
1806-1819 300-302	906		2469-70	1810-1819 1476-1478		
1806-1820 303-304	907	1211	2471-2	1809-1819 1479-1480		
		1211				
1795-1815 305		1212				
		1212				
1795-1811 306-307		1213				

REGIMENTS OF FOOT GUARDS	MUSTER BOOKS & PAY LISTS		REGIMENTAL REGISTERS	
	Years	WO12/	Marriages Years	Birth/Bapt Years
1st (1656)	1732,40-1	1537-1538	see Quebec Garrison	
Grenadier Guards	1760-1877	1539-1656	Vols 5 & 6	
2nd (1650)	1759-1877	1657-1770	1876-1915	1876-1915
Coldstream Guards				
3rd (1662)	1762-1877	1771-1881	1796-1838	1804-1892
Scots Guards			1861-1892	
4th (1900)			1890-1913	1890-1913
Irish Guards				
5th (1915)				
Welsh Guards				

REGIMENTS OF INFANTRY
Best known pre-1914 titles
given with dates of original
formation and renaming

Foot	Bn	Years	WO12/	Marriages	Birth/Bapt
1 (1633/1678)	1	1768-1877	1882-1947	1840-1903	1843-1903
Royal Regiment (1684)	2	1759-1877	1948-2009	1842-1907	1844-1907
Royal Scots (1812)	3	1804-1817	2010-2014		
Lothian (Royal Scots)(1881)	4	1805-1816	2015-2019		
	Dep			1885-1908	1885-1908
2 (1661/1684)	1	1768-1877	2020-2083	1833-1908	1854-1908
Queen's Royal (1703)	2	1857-1877	2084-2103	1845-1913	1846-1913
West Surrey (1881)	Dep			1833-1908	1834-1908
3 (1665/1689)	1	1760-1877	2104-2167	1849-1907	1860-1908
Buffs (1702/1751)	2	1803-1877	2168-2193	1844-1908	1838-1908
East Kent (1881)	3			(1829-1877	1841-1888?)
	Dep			1829-1877	1841-1888
4 (1680)	1	1764-1877	2194-2259	1821-1914	1830-1914
King's Own (1715)	2	*1799-1877	2260-2286	1839-1907	1845-1908
Royal Lancaster (1881)	3	1799-1802	2287-2288	1885-1908	1885-1908
	4			1881-1912	1881-1912
5 (1674/1688)	1	1760-1877	2289-2352	1798-1914	1812-1914
Northumberland (1782)	2	*1799-1877	2353-2379	1845-1914	1849-1914
Northumberland Fusiliers (1836)	3			1886-1912	1886-1912
	4			1879-1911	1879-1911
6 (1674/1688)	1	1760-1877	2380-2447	1835-1907	1846-1907
1st Warwickshire (1782)	2	*1805-1877	2448-2473	1842-1907	1844-1907
Royal 1st Warwickshire (1832)	3			1826-1906	1826-1906
Royal Warwickshire (1881)	4			1835-1907	1835-1907
	Mil			1867-1909	1867-1909

*(gap from 1816-1856)

REGIMENTAL RECORDS

DESCRIPTION AND SUCCESSION BOOKS Years WO25/ (uos)	SERVICE RETURNS No 1 WO25/	MMG's Cas. Index WO25/	INDEX TO CASUALTY RETURNS WO25/	CASUALTY RETURNS Years WO25/	SOLDIERS' DOCUMENTS (Bn not specified) 1760-1854 WO97/	1855-1872 WO97/
	874		(2475 (	1823-1850 1487-1488	(150 (	1365-1371
	875		(& (	1823-1850 1489-1490	(to	1372-1376
Depot: WO 67/ 1768-1830 1-6	876		((2476	1823-1850 1491-1493	((218	1377-1381
1798-1832 308-311	909		1216 (2477	1809-1830 1494-1498	219- 239	1382-1386
1806-1831 312-313	910		1217-8 (	1809-1831 1499-1505		
1812-1817 314-315			1219 (to	1809-1817 1506		
1798-1816 316-317	911		1219 (2481	1809-1816 1507		
				1825-1831 1508		
1811-1843 318-321	912		1220	2482 2483 1810-1845 1509-1515	240- 247	1387-1389
1804-1831 322-324	913		1221	2484 1809-1845 1516-1519	248- 258	1390-1393
1807-1816 325-326	914			2485 1809-1815 1520		
1823-1833 327-328				1825-1827 1521		
	915		1222	2486 1809-1847 1522-1526	259- 267	1394-1397
	916		1223 1224	2487 1809-1815 1527		
				(1825-1828 1528:Depot)		
	917		1225	2488 1809-1830 1529-1533	268- 276	1398-1400
	918		1226	2489 1809-1816 1535		
				(1825-1826 1534:Depot)		
1804-1812 329	919		1227	2490 1809-1842 1536-1542	277- 286	1401-1403
	920			2491 1809-1816 1543		

Depot: WO 67/
1890-1908 28-29

REGIMENTS OF INFANTRY Best known pre-1914 titles given with dates of original formation and renaming Foot	Bn	MUSTER BOOKS & PAY LISTS Years WO12/		REGIMENTAL REGISTERS Marriages Years	Birth/Bapt Years
7 (1685) Royal Fusiliers (1751) City of London (1881)	1 2	1760-1877 1781-1798 1804-1815 1857-1877	2474-2565 2475&2541 2541-2545 2546-2565	1871-1908 1877-1908	1871-1908 1877-1908
	Mil			1848-1908	1848-1908
8 (1685) The King's (1751) Liverpool (1881)	1 2	1760-1877 1805-1815 1857-1877	2566-2627 2628-2632 2633-2652	1824-1908 1844-1907	1834-1908 1848-1907
	4 Mil			1867-1908 1836-1903	1867-1908 1836-1903
9 (1685) (East) Norfolk (1782) Norfolk (1881)	1 2 3	1760-1777 1781-1877 1799-1815 1857-1877 1799-1802	2653 2654-2721 2722-2727 2728-2747 2748-2749	1855-1914 1873-1914	1858-1914 1873-1914
	Mil			1825-1899	1827-1905
10 (1685) (North) Lincolnshire (1782) Lincolnshire (1881)	1 2 3	1767-1877 1804-1816 1858-1877	2750-2814 2815-2818 2819-2837	1840-1909 1852-1909 1878-1924	1845-1909 1852-1909 1878-1924
11 (1685) (North) Devonshire (1782) Devonshire (1881)	1 2 3	1760-1877 1808-1816 1857-1858 1858-1877	2838-2909 2910-2912 2890 2913-2933	1839-1908 1825-1907	1839-1908 1834-1907
	Mil			1827-1906	1834-1905
12 (1685) (East) Suffolk (1782) Suffolk (1881)	1 2 4	1760-1877 1812-1818 1857-1877	2934-3004 3005-3006 3007-3027	1802-1913 1809-1871 1876-1913	1814-1913 1818-1870 1876-1913
	Mil			1887-1909	1887-1909
13 (1685) 1st Somersetshire (1782) Somerset Light Infantry (1822) Prince Albert's (1842)	1 2 Mil	1760-1877 1857-1858 1858-1877	3028-3097 3077 3098-3116	1799-1914 1873-1906 1875-1922	1790-1914 1873-1906 1875-1922
14 (1685) Bedfordshire (1782) Buckinghamshire (1809) Prince of Wales's Own (1876) West Yorkshire (1881)	1 2 3 Mil	1760-1877 1804-1818 1857-1858 1858-1877 1814-1816	3117-3197 3198-3203 3174 3204-3226 3227	1814-1919 1873-1919 1884-1914	1818-1919 1873-1919 1884-1914
15 (1685) Yorkshire East Riding (1782) East Yorkshire (1881)	1 2	1759-1876 1799-1816 1857-1858 1858-1877	3228-3293 3294-3300 3275 3301-3319	1821-1913 1841-1899	1829-1913 1844-1878

DESCRIPTION AND SUCCESSION BOOKS Years	WO25/ (uos)	SERVICE RETURNS No 1 WO25/	MMG's Cas. Index WO25/	INDEX TO CASUALTY RETURNS WO25/	CASUALTY RETURNS Years	WO25/	SOLDIERS' DOCUMENTS (Bn not specified) 1760-1854 WO97/	1855-1872 WO97/
		921	1228	2492	1809-1830	1544-1546	287- 293	1404-1408
1848-1864	330	922		2493	1809-1815	1548		
					(1825-1830	1547:Depot)		
		923	1229	2494	1809-1830	1549-1553	294- 301	1409-1412
		924		2495	1809-1815	1554		
					(1830	1555:Reserve)		
Depot: 1806-1853 WO67/7								
		925	1230	2496	1809-1844	1556-1560	302- 312	1413-1415
		926	1231	2497	1809-1816	1561		
			1232		(1825-1826	1562:Depot)		
1809-1827	331-332	927	1233	2498	1809-1830	1563-1566	313- 321	1416-1419
		928		2499	1809-1816	1567		
					(1826-1830	1568:Depot)		
1816-1829	333	929	1234	2500	1809-1831	1569-1571	322- 331	1420-1423
				2501	1809-1816	1572		
					(1826-1830	1573:Depot)		
1814-1830	334-336	930	1235	2502	1809-1830	1574-1578	332- 340	1424-1427
				2503	1811-1817	1579		
					(1825-1830	1580:Depot)		
		931	1236	2504	1809-1845	1581-1590	341- 348	1428-1431
				2505				
1791-1812	337-338	932	1237	2506	1810-1831	1591-1596	349- 360	1432-1435
1805-1818	339	933		2507	1809-1817	1597		
1813-1816	340				1813-1816	1598		
1818-1823	341 (Depot)							
		934	1238	2508	1809-1830	1599-1602	361- 367	1436-1439
		935	1239	2509	1809-1816	1603		
					(1827-1830	1604:Depot)		

REGIMENTS OF INFANTRY Best known pre-1914 titles given with dates of original formation and renaming		MUSTER BOOKS & PAY LISTS		REGIMENTAL REGISTERS	
Foot	Bn	Years	WO12/	Marriages Years	Birth/Bapt Years
16 (1688)	1	1767-1877	3320-3385	1809-1914	1819-1914
Bedfordshire (1809)	2	1857-1877	3386-3404	1858-1876	1859-1877
17 (1688)	1	1760-1877	3405-3479	1809-1909	1809-1909
Leicestershire (1782)	2	1799-1802	3480-3481	1838-1908	1846-1908
		1858-1877	3482-3500		
	Mil/3			1832-1904	1842-1905
18 (1684)	1	1767-1877	3501-3567	1865-1897	1865-1897
Royal Irish (ca 1751)	2	1803-1814	3568-3572		
		1858-1877	3573-3591		
19 (1688)	1	1760-1877	3592-3654	1823-1906	1845-1906
Princess of Wales's Own Yorkshire	2	1858-1877	3655-3674		
(1881), Green Howards (1921)	Mil/3			1840-1902	1852-1900
20 (1688)	1	1760-1877	3675-3750	1853-1906	1858-1906
East Devonshire (1782)	2	1799-1802	3751-3753	1867-1899	1870-1901
Lancashire Fusiliers (1881)		1858-1877	3754-3777		
	Mil/3			1841-1913	1842-1913
21 (1678)	1	1760-1877	3778-3845	1826-1907	1844-1907
Royal North British Fuzileers	2	1804-1816	3846-3850	1846-1894	1852-1896
(1751)		1858-1877	3851-3870		
Royal Scots Fusiliers (1877)	Mil/3			1852-1907	1855-1908
22 (1689)	1	1760-1877	3871-3938	1798-1908	1802-1908
Cheshire (1751)	2	1814	3939	1839-1908	1844-1908
		1858-1877	3940-3958	1839-1908	1844-1908
23 (1689)	1	1760-1877	3959-4035	1808-1908	1805-1908
Royal Welch Fusiliers (1727)	2	1805-1814	4036-4039		
		1858-1877	4040-4058		
24 (1689)	1	1760-1877	4059-4132	1803-1908	1804-1908
2nd Warwickshire (1782)	2	1804-1814	4133-4138	1871-1906	1871-1906
South Wales Borderers (1881)		1858-1877	4139-4157		
25 (1689)	1	1760-1877	4158-4225	1823-1908	1827-1908
King's Own Borderers (1805)	2	1804-1816	4226-4232	1877-1907	1877-1907
King's Own Scottish Borderers (1887)		1859-1877	4233-4249		
26 (1689)	1	1766-1877	4250-4319	1792-1908	1793-1908
Cameronians (1786)	2	1803-1814	4320-4327		
(Scottish Rifles 1881) see 90th	Dep				
27 (1689)	1	1759-1857	4328-4398	1857-1908	1862-1908
Inniskilling (1751)	2	1800-1817	4399-4408		
Royal Inniskilling Fusiliers	3	1805-1816	4409-4415		
(1881) see 108th	Mil			1880-1917	1880-1917
28 (1694)	1	1759-1877	4416-4484	1823-1906	1832-1903
North Gloucestershire (1782)	2	1803-1814	4485-4492		
Gloucestershire (1881)	Dep				
see 61st	Dep				
29 (1694)	1	1765-1877	4493-4560	1826-1907	1836-1907
Worcestershire (1782) see 36th	2	1784-1797	4494		

DESCRIPTION AND SUCCESSION BOOKS Years WO25/ (uos)	SERVICE RETURNS No 1 WO25/	MMG's Cas. Index WO25/	INDEX TO CASUALTY RETURNS WO25/	CASUALTY RETURNS Years	WO25/	SOLDIERS' DOCUMENTS (Bn not specified) 1760-1854 WO97/	1855-1872 WO97/
	936	1240	2510	1809-1840	1605-1611	368- 376	1440-1443
			2511	(1825-1828	1612:Depot)		
	937	1241	2512	1810-1847	1613-1617	377- 384	1444-1446
		1242	2513				
Depot: WO67/ 1830-1887 8-11							
1806-1851 342-343	938	1243	2514	1810-1845	1618-1620	385- 392	1447-1450
	939		2515	1809-1814	1621		
				(1825-1830	1622:Depot)		
	940	1244	2516	1809-1830	1623-1626	393- 400	1451-1455
			2517				
				(1826-1830	1627:Depot)		
1809-1831 344-346	941	1245	2518	1809-1836	1628-1632	401- 408	1456-1459
		1246	2519				
Depot: WO67/ 1823-1881 12-13							
	942	1247	2520	1809-1848	1633-1637	409- 417	1460-1463
	943		2521	1809-1816	1638		
				(1825-1828	1639:Depot)		
	944	1248	2522	1809-1855	1640-1644	418- 425	1464-1467
			2523				
				(1826-1830	1645:Depot)		
1814-1830 347-349	945	1249	2524	1809-1830	1646-1649	426- 433	1468-1471
1809-1817 350	946		2525	1809-1814	1650		
				(1825-1830	1651:Depot)		
	947	1250	2526	1809-1830	1652-1656	434- 441	1472-1475
Depot: WO67/	948		2527	1808-1814	1657		
1881-1897 30-31				(1829-1830	1658:Depot)		
1810-1818 351	949	1251	2528	1809-1842	1659-1661	442- 450	1476-1479
1809-1818 352	950		2529	1809-1816	1662		
				(1825-1830	1663:Depot)		
1803-1843 353-354	951	1252	2530	1809-1843	1664-1669	451- 458	1480-1483
	952		2531	1809-1815	1670		
1850-1858 355							
1816-1829 356	953	1253	2532	1810-1830	1671-1673	459- 468	1484-1485
	954	1254	2533	1809-1817	1674		
		1254	2534	1809-1816	1675		
				(1825-1830	1676:Depot)		
1795-1806 357	955	1255	2535	1809-1847	1677-1681	469- 476	1486-1487
1803-1830 358-362	956		2536	1809-1814	1682		
1806 363				1825-1830	1683		
1792-1866 WO67/24-27							
1826-1831 364	957	1256	2537	1809-1830	1684-1687	477- 483	1488-1489
			2538	(1826-1830	1688:Depot)		

REGIMENTS OF INFANTRY Best known pre-1914 titles given with dates of original formation and renaming Foot	Bn	MUSTER BOOKS & PAY LISTS Years	WO12/	REGIMENTAL REGISTERS Marriages Years	Birth/Bapt Years
30 (1702), 1st Cambridgeshire see (1782), East Lancashire (1881) 59th	1 2	1760-1877 1803-1817	4561-4639 4640-4647	1791-1908	1803-1908
31 (1702), Huntingdonshire (1782) East Surrey (1881) see 70th	1 2	1760-1877 1805-1814	4648-4719 4720-4724	1841-1909	1852-1909
32 (1702), Cornwall (1782) Duke of Cornwall's Light Infantry (1881) see 46th	1 2 Dep	1760-1877 1804-1814 1857-1858	4725-4796 4797-4801 4700	1846-1908	1853-1908
33 (1702), 1st Yorkshire West Riding (1782), Duke of Wellington's (1853) see 76th	1 2 Dep	1760-1877	4802-4865	1803-1913	1810-1913
34 (1702) Cumberland (1782) Border (1881) see 55th	1 2 Dep	1760-1877 1805-1817	4866-4942 4943-4948	1838-1907	1845-1907
35 (1701) Dorsetshire (1782) Sussex (1805) Royal Sussex (1832) see 107th	1 2 Dep	1759-1877 1770 1799-1817	4949-5015 6710 5016-5024	1854-1908	1857-1908
36 (1701) Herefordshire (1782) 2nd Bn Worcestershire (1881)	1 2 Dep	1760-1877 1804-1814	5025-5095 5096-5099	1799-1909	1801-1909
37 (1702) North Hampshire (1782) Hampshire (1881) see 67th	1 2 Dep	1760-1877 1813-1817	5100-5168 5169-5170	1824-1906	1811-1906
38 (1705) 1st Staffordshire (1782) South Staffordshire (1881) see 80th	1 2	1760-1877 1805-1814	5171-5240 5241-5245	1819-1909	1830-1909
39 (1702) East Middlesex (1782) Dorsetshire (1807/1881) see 54th	1 2 Dep	1769-1877 1803-1815	5246-5309 5310-5316	1834-1908	1844-1908
40 (1717), 2nd Somersetshire (1782) Prince of Wales's Volunteers (South Lancashire) (1881) see 82nd	1 2 Dep	1759-1877 1799-1815	5317-5396 5397-5403	1799-1908	1804-1908
41 (1719), The Welsh (1831) The Welch (1881) see 69th	1 2	1760-1877 1812-1813	5404-5476 5477	1810-1908	1816-1908
42 (1738) Royal Highland (1758) The Black Watch (1861) (Royal Highlanders - 1881) see 73rd	1 2 Dep	1759-1877 1759-1783 1803-1814	5478-5552 5553 5554-5560	1825-1880	1832-1880
43 (1739), Monmouthshire (1782) Oxfordshire Light Infantry (1881) (and Bucks - 1908) see 52nd	1 2 Dep/3	1759-1877 1804-1817	5561-5630 5631-5636	1811-1908 1796-1849	1814-1908 1803-1849
44 (1739), East Essex (1782) Essex (1881) see 56th	1 2	1759-1877 1803-1816	5637-5710 5711-5717	1852-1913	1854-1913
45 (1739), Nottinghamshire (1779) Sherwood Foresters/Derbys. (1881)	1 2	1759-1877 1804-1814	5718-5791 5792-5795	1876-1909 (see 95th Foot)	1876-1909

REGIMENTAL RECORDS

DESCRIPTION AND SUCCESSION BOOKS Years	WO25/ (uos)	SERVICE RETURNS No 1 WO25/	MMG's Cas. Index WO25/	INDEX TO CASUALTY RETURNS WO25/	CASUALTY RETURNS Years	WO25/	SOLDIERS' DOCUMENTS (Bn not specified) 1760-1854 WO97/	1855-1872 WO97/
		958	1257	2539	1809-1830	1689-1694	484- 493	1490-1492
		959		2540	1809-1817	1695		
1814-1818	365	960	1258	2541	1809-1846	1696-1704	494- 503	1493-1494
				2542	1809-1814	1705		
1815-1829	366-367	961	1259	2543	1809-1830	1706-1708	504- 509	1495-1496
1808-1816	368	962		2544	1809-1814	1709		
					1825-1830	1710		
1813-1825	369	963	1260	2545	1809-1830	1711-1715	510- 515	1497-1499
				2546				
					1825-1830	1716		
		964	1261	2547	1809-1830	1717-1721	516- 520	1500-1502
		965		2548	1809-1817	1722		
1803-1873	WO67/14				1829-1830	1723		
1811-1823	370-372	966	(1262	2549	1809-1830	1724-1728	521- 528	1503-1504
			(1263					
		967		2550	1809-1817	1729		
1817-1832	373				1825-1830	1730		
1804-1838	374-375	968	1264	2551	1809-1830	1731-1734	529- 535	1505-1506
		969		2552	1809-1814	1735		
1840-1857	376				1825-1830	1736		
		970	1265	2553	1809-1830	1737-1739	536- 542	1507-1508
				2554	1813-1817	1740		
					1825-1830	1741		
1790-1831	377	971	1266	2555	1809-1836	1742-1749	543- 549	1509-1511
1848-1868	378							
		972		2556	1809-1814	1750		
		973	1267	2557	1809-1847	1751-1757	550- 558	1512-1513
	WO67/	974		2558	1809-1816	1758		
1857-1892	15-16				1827-1828	1759		
		975	1268	2559	1809-1845	1760-1765	559- 567	1514-1515
			1269	2560	1809-1815	1766		
1824-1865	WO67/17				1827	1767		
		976	1270	2561	1810-1843	1768-1776	568- 575	1516-1518
				2562	1813	1777		
1795-1816	379-383	977	1271	2563	1809-1830	1778-1780	576- 582	1519-1521
1803-1805	384	978		2564	1809-1814	1781		
1825-1830	385				1825-1830	1782		
1818-1838	386-388	979	1272	2565	1809-1830	1783-1785	583- 590	1522-1524
		980	1272	2566	1809-1816	1786		
			1273		(1825-1830	1787:Depot)		
		981	1274	2567	1809-1842	1788-1794	591- 596	1525-1527
		982		2568	1809-1816	1795		
1815-1832	389-392	983	1275	2569	1809-1837	1796-1806	597- 602	1528-1531
(1826-32	393:Dep)	984		2570	1809-1814	1807		

REGIMENTS OF INFANTRY Best known pre-1914 titles given with dates of original formation and renaming Foot	Bn	MUSTER BOOKS & PAY LISTS Years WO12/	REGIMENTAL REGISTERS Marriages Years	Birth/Bapt Years
46 (1739), South Devonshire (1782) 2nd Bn Duke of Cornwall's Light Infantry (1881)	1 2 Dep	1761-1877 5796-5867 1800-1802 5868-5870	1815-1906	1821-1906
47 (1739), Lancashire (1782) see Loyal North Lancashire (1881) 81st	1 2	1759-1877 5871-5948 1803-1816 5949-5956	1798-1913	1804-1913
48 (1739) see Northamptonshire (1782/1881) 58th	1 2	1759-1877 5957-6024 1803-1814 6025-6031	1868-1914	1868-1914
49 (1739), Hertfordshire (1782) Princess Charlotte of Wales's (1816), Berkshire (1881) see 66th	1 2 Dep	1774-1877 6032-6100 1813-1814 6101	1826-1908	1818-1908
50 (1739), West Kent (1782) Queen's Own (1831) see 97th Queen's Own (Royal West Kent) (1881)	1 2 Dep	1760-1877 6102-6170 1804-1814 6171-6175	1844-1908	1839-1908
51 (1739), 2nd Yorkshire West Riding (1782), King's Own Yorkshire Light Infantry (1887) see 105th	1 2 Dep	1756-1877 6176-6239	1848-1914	1854-1914
52 (1739), Oxfordshire (1782) 2nd Bn Oxfords Light Inf (1881) (and Buckinghamshire - 1908)	1 2 Dep	1765-1877 6240-6306 1799-1816 6307-6315	1798-1907	1802-1907
53 (1739), Shropshire (1782) The King's (Shropshire Light Infantry) (1882) see 85th	1 2 Dep	1760-1877 6316-6388 1803-1817 6389-6397	1803-1908	1804-1908
54 (1741) West Norfolk (1782) 2nd Bn Dorsetshire (1881)	1 2	1760-1861 6398-6450 1861-1862 6526 1862-1877 6452-6468 1800-1802 6469	1794-1907	1812-1907
55 (1741) Westmoreland (1782) 2nd Bn Border (1881)	1 2	1759-1861 6470-6525 1861-1862 6451 1862-1877 6527-6542	1797-1908	1799-1908
56 (1741) West Essex (1782) 2nd Bn Essex (1881)	1 2 3 Dep	1760-1877 6543-6619 1804-1817 6620-6630 1813-1814 6631	1856-1914	1858-1914
57 (1741) West Middlesex (1782) Duke of Cambridge's Own (Middlesex) (1881) see 77th	1 2 Dep/&c Dep	1760-1877 6632-6704 1803-1815 6705-6709	1799-1921	1802-1921
58 (1741) Rutlandshire (1782) 2nd Bn Northamptonshire (1881)	1 2 Dep Res	1759-1877 6710-6779 1804-1815 6780-6785	1878-1916	1878-1916
59 (1741), 2nd Nottinghamshire (1782), 2nd Bn East Lancs (1881)	1 2	1765-1877 6786-6864 1805-1816 6865-6870	1795-1905	1804-1905

DESCRIPTION AND SUCCESSION BOOKS Years	WO25/ (uos)	SERVICE RETURNS No 1 WO25/	MMG's Cas. Index WO25/	INDEX TO CASUALTY RETURNS WO25/	CASUALTY RETURNS Years	WO25/	SOLDIERS' DOCUMENTS (Bn not specified) 1760-1854 WO97/	1855-1872 WO97/
1810-1856	394-398	985	1276	2571	1809-1833	1808-1816	603- 610	1532-1534
				2572				
1813-1864	399-402							
		986	1277	2573	1809-1830	1817-1821	611- 621	1535-1537
		987		2574	1809-1816	1822		
1812-1825	403-404	988	1278	2575	1809-1834	1823-1827	622- 628	1538-1540
				2576	1809-1814	1828		
		989	1279	2577	1810-1843	1829-1834	629- 635	1541-1543
				2578	1813-1814	1835		
					1825-1828	1836		
		990	1280	2579	1809-1848	1837-1840	636- 644	1544-1546
		991		2580	1810-1814	1841		
					1825-1827	1842		
		992	1281	2581	1809-1854	1843-1848	645- 652	1547-1549
				2582				
					1825-1830	1849		
1783-1829	405-407	993	1282	2583	1809-1856	1850-1854	653- 661	1550-1551
1807-1821	408-410	994		2584	1809-1816	1855		
1824-1830	411				1825-1830	1856		
1795-1825	412-414	995	1283	2585	1817-1855	1857-1865	662- 668	1552-1553
1803-1818	415-416			2586	1809-1817	1866		
1807-1859	417-419				1829-1830	1867		
1801-1812	420	996	1284	2587	1809-1840	1868-1875	669- 677	1554-1556
			1285	2588				
1814-1832	421-423	997	1286	2589	1809-1843	1876-1883	678- 687	1557-1559
				2590	(1825-1830	1884:Depot)		
		998	1287	2591	1810-1830	1885-1889	688- 695	1560-1561
		999		2592	1810-1817	1890		
					1814	1891		
					1825-1826	1892		
1820-1840	424-425	1000	1288	2593	1809-1846	1893-1897	696- 704	1562-1564
1803-1821	426-428	1001		2594	1809-1815	1898		
1806-1877	429-433							
1854-1866	434				1825-1827	1899		
1756-1830	435-442	1002	1289	2595	1809-1830	1900-1903	705- 712	1565-1566
1806-1815	443-444	1003		2596	1809-1815	1904		
1816-1825	445				1827-1830	1905		
1818-1831	446							
		1004	1290	2597	1809-1830	1906-1910	713- 723	1567-1568
				2598	1809-1816	1911		

REGIMENTAL RECORDS

REGIMENTS OF INFANTRY Best known pre-1914 titles given with dates of original formation and renaming Foot	Bn	MUSTER BOOKS & PAY LISTS Years	WO12/	REGIMENTAL REGISTERS Marriages Years	Birth/Bapt Years
60 (1741)	1	1763-1877	6871-6934	1832-1913	1833-1913
Royal American Regiment (1756)	2	1764-1877	6935-6997	1812-1891	1810-1892
Duke of York's Rifle Corps (1824)	3	1757-1819	6998-7009		
The King's Royal Rifle Corps		1855-1877	7010-7032		
Regiment of Foot (1830)	4	1757-1819	7033-7044		
The King's Royal Rifle Corps (1881)		1857-1877	7045-7064		
	5	1798-1818	7065-7076		
	6	1799-1818	7077-7087		
	7	1813-1818	7088-7089		
	8	1814-1816	7090		
	Dep				
61 (1739)	1	1760-1877	7091-7157	1802-1907	1808-1907
South Gloucestershire (1782)	2	1803-1814	7158-7163		
2nd Bn Gloucestershire (1881)	Dep				
62 (1742), Wiltshire (1782) see	1	1772-1877	7164-7232	1867-1908	1867-1908
Duke of Edinburgh's (1881) 99th	2	1799-1817	7233-7240		
63 (1743)	1	1771-1877	7241-7307	1833-1906	1839-1912
West Suffolk (1782)	2	1804-1814	7308-7311	1892-1907	1892-1907
Manchester (1881) see 96th	Dep				
64 (1745), 2nd Staffordshire	1	1760-1877	7312-7376	1843-1908	1847-1908
(1782), Prince of Wales's (North					
Staffordshire) (1881) see 98th	Dep				
65 (1745)	1	1768-1877	7377-7457	1858-1914	1807-1914
2nd Yorkshire (North Riding) (1782)					
York and Lancaster (1881) see 84th	Dep				
66 (1745), Berkshire (1782)	1	1759-1877	7458-7527	1839-1909	1845-1909
2nd Bn Princess Charlotte of	2	1803-1817	7528-7535		
Wales's (Royal Berkshire) (1885)					
67 (1745)	1	1760-1877	7536-7615	1830-1906	1832-1906
South Hampshire (1782)	2	1804-1817	7616-7621		
2nd Bn Hampshire (1881)	Dep				
68 (1745)	1	1760-1877	7622-7689	1852-1914	1853-1914
Durham (1782) see 106th	2	1800-1802	7690-7692		
Durham Light Infantry (1808/1881)	Dep				
69 (1745)	1	1760-1877	7693-7772	1800-1907	1807-1907
South Lincolnshire (1782)	2	1795	7695		
2nd Bn The Welch (1881)		1803-1816	7773-7779		
	Dep				
70 (1745), Surrey (1782), Glasgow	1	1774-1877	7780-7846	1810-1908	1811-1908
Lowland (1813), Surrey (1825)					
2nd Bn East Surrey (1881)	Dep				
71 (1745), Highland (1786) see	1	1764-1877	7847-7918	1798-1908	1798-1908
Glasgow Highland (1808) 74th	2	1776-1783	7847		
Highland Light Infantry (ca 1810)		1805-1816	7919-7923		
	Dep				

DESCRIPTION AND SUCCESSION BOOKS Years	WO25/ (uos)	SERVICE RETURNS No 1 WO25/	MMG's Cas. Index WO25/	INDEX TO CASUALTY RETURNS WO25/	CASUALTY RETURNS Years	WO25/	SOLDIERS' DOCUMENTS (Bn not specified) 1760-1854 WO97/	1855-1872 WO97/
		1005	1291	2599	1809-1830	1912-1914	724- 745	1569-1575
1854	447	1006	1292	2600	1809-1830	1915-1917		
			1293	2601	1809-1819	1918-1919		
		1007	1294	2602	1809-1819	1920-1921		
		1008	1295	2603	1809-1817	1922		
		1009	1296		1810-1817	1923		
			1296		1813-1817	1924		
			1296		1810-1817	1925		
					1826-1830	1926-1927		
		1010	1297	2604	1809-1850	1928-1932	746- 752	1576-1578
		1011		2605	1809-1814	1933		
					1827-1830	1934		
		1012	1298	2606	1809-1847	1935-1941	753- 760	1579-1580
		1013	1299	2607	1809-1817	1942		
		1014	1300	2608	1809-1817	1943-1948	761- 771	1581-1582
		1015		2609	1809-1814	1949		
					1826-1828	1950		
1797-1800	448	1016	1301	2610	1809-1854	1951-1954	772- 781	1583-1585
1814-1816	449			2611				
					1826-1827	1955		
		1017	1302	2612	1809-1830	1956-1960	782- 788	1586-1587
				2613				
1826-1873	WO67/18				1829-1830	1961		
1825-1865	450-452	1018	1303	2614	1803-1830	1962-1966	789- 797	1588-1590
		1019		2615	1809-1817	1967		
					1827-1830	1968		
1806-1817	453	1020	1304	2616	1809-1830	1969-1974	798- 806	1591-1593
				2617	1809-1817	1975		
					1825-1826	1976		
		1021	1305	2618	1809-1830	1977-1979	807- 815	1594-1596
			1306	2619				
	WO67/							
1873-1901	21-23				1825-1829	1980		
1826-1830	454-455	1022	1307	2620	1809-1830	1981-1985	816- 823	1597-1598
and 1855				2621	1809-1817	1986		
					1825-1826	1987		
		1023	1308	2622	1809-1854	1988-1992	824- 829	1599-1600
				2623				
					1825-1827	1993		
1809-1818	456-457	1024	1309	2624	1809-1830	1994-1997	830- 838	1601-1602
1810-1822	458-460	1025		2625	1809-1815	1998		
					1825-1830	1999		

REGIMENTS OF INFANTRY Best known pre-1914 titles given with dates of original formation and renaming Foot	Bn	MUSTER BOOKS & PAY LISTS Years	WO12/	REGIMENTAL REGISTERS Marriages Years	Birth/Bapt Years
72 (1745), Highland (1786) see 78th Duke of Albany's Own Highlanders (1823), Seaforth Highlanders (1881)	1 2 Dep	1764-1877 1804-1816	7924-7991 7992-7996	1808-1908	1806-1808
73 (1745), Highland (1786), Perthshire (1862), 2nd Bn Black Watch (Royal Highlanders) (1881)	1 2 Res/Dep	1764-1877 1779-1817	7997-8058 8059-8062	1792-1873	1799-1874
74 (1745), Highland (1787), Assaye (1803), 2nd Bn Highland Light Infantry (1881)	1 Dep	1763-1877	8063-8128	1797-1907	1810-1907
75 (1745), Abercromby's Highlanders (1787), Stirlingshire (1862) Gordon Highlanders (1881) see 92nd	1 Res	1763-1877	8129-8190	1839-1909	1844-1909
76 (1745), Hindoostan (to 1812) 2nd Bn Duke of Wellington's (West Riding Regiment) (1881)	1 Dep	1778-1877	8191-8253	1853-1914	1863-1914
77 (1745), East Middlesex (1807) 2nd Bn Duke of Cambridge's Own (Middlesex Regiment) (1881)	1	1778-1877	8254-8313	1830-1908	1837-1908
78 (1745), Highland (1793) Ross-shire Buffs (1794/6), 2nd Bn Seaforth Highlanders (Ross-Shire Buffs, The Duke of Albany's) (1881)	1 2 Dep	1778-1785 1793-1802 1806-1877 1804-1816	8314 8314 8315-8373 8374-8379	1793-1908	1806-1908
79 (1745), Cameron Highlanders (1804), Queen's Own Cameron Highlanders (1873)	1 2 Res/Dep	1780 1794-1877 1804-1815	8380 8380-8448 8449-8453	1794-1909	1795-1909
80 (1758) Staffordshire Volunteers (1793) 2nd Bn South Staffordshire Regiment (1881)	1 Dep	1778-1784 1793-1797 1808-1877	8454 8455 8456-8518	1854-1908	1853-1908
81 (1758) Loyal Lincolnshire Volunteers (1793) 2nd Bn Loyal North Lancashire Regiment (1881)	1 2 Dep	1760-1763 1778-1783 1794-1877 1803-1816	8519 8520-8521 8522-8588 8589-8596	1816-1906	1802-1906
82 (1758) Prince of Wales's Volunteers (1793) 2nd Bn Prince of Wales's Volunteers (South Lancashire) (1881)	1 2 Dep	1760-1763 1778-1784 1793-1877 1794-1795 1804-1815	8597 8597 8597-8665 8666 8667-8670	1805-1907	1815-1907
83 (1758), Fitch's Grenadiers (1793), County of Dublin (1859) 2nd Bn Royal Irish Rifles (1881)	1 2 Dep	1778-1877 1804-1817	8671-8734 8735-8740	1876-1914	1876-1914

DESCRIPTION AND SUCCESSION BOOKS Years WO25/ (uos)	SERVICE RETURNS No 1 WO25/	MMG's Cas. Index WO25/	INDEX TO CASUALTY RETURNS WO25/	CASUALTY RETURNS Years	WO25/	SOLDIERS' DOCUMENTS (Bn not specified) 1760-1854 WO97/	1855-1872 WO97/
1801-1808 461)	1026	1310	2626	1809-1831	2000-2002	839- 846	1603-1604
1812-1822 462)	1027		2627	1809-1815	2003		
				1827-1830	2004		
1786-1867 463)	1028	1311	2628	1809-1830	2005-2008	847- 857	1605-1606
1809-1872 465-6)			2629	1809-1817	2009		
1809-1841 464 (Res & Dep)				1827-1830	2010 (Dep)		
1810-1830 467-470	1029	1312	2630 2631	1810-1830	2011-2014	858- 864	1607-1609
1853-1868 WO67/19				1825-1830	2015		
1778-1783 471-472	1030	1313	2632 2633	1809-1831	2016-2019	865- 871	1610-1612
				1830	2020		
	1031	1314	2634 2635	1809-1830	2021-2023	872- 877	1613-1615
				1825-1829	2024		
1811-1833 473-476	1032	1315	2636 2637	1809-1831	2025-2028	878- 884	1616-1618
	1033	1316	2638 2639	1809-1850	2029-2037	885- 890	1619-1621
	1034			1809-1816	2038		
				1826-1830	2039		
1809-1842 477,479	1035	1317	2640 2641	1809-1830	2040-2043	891- 897	1622-1623
1809-1842 478,479	1036			1809-1815	2044		
1809-1850 480 (Res)				1825-1830	2045 (Dep)		
1804-1881 Descr. Book held at RHQ Staffordshire Reg Lichfield	1037	1318	2642 2643	1810-1854	2046-2054	898- 904	1624-1625
				1825-1830	2055		
1801-1863 481-487	1038	1319	2644 2645	1809-1830	2056-2058	905- 913	1626-1628
				1809-1816	2059		
1839-1863 488				1825-1830	2060		
1799-1831 489-492	1039	1320	2646 2647	1809-1830	2061-2063	914- 922	1629-1630
1804-1817 493-494	1040			1809-1815	2064		
				1825-1830	2065		
1812-1868 495-497	1041 1042	1321	2648 2649	1809-1830	2066-2070	923- 932	1631-1633
				1809-1817	2071		
				1825-1830	2072		

REGIMENTS OF INFANTRY Best known pre-1914 titles given with dates of original formation and renaming Foot	Bn	MUSTER BOOKS & PAY LISTS Years WO12/	REGIMENTAL REGISTERS Marriages Years	Birth/Bapt Years
84 (1758)	1	1780-1877 8741-8805	1820-1914	1822-1914
York and Lancaster (1809)	2	1779-1796 8806		
2nd Bn York and Lancaster (1881)		1808-1817 8807-8811		
	Dep			
85 (1759), Bucks Volunteers (1793)	1	1780-1783 8812	1829-1906	1844-1906
King's Light Infantry (1821), 2nd Bn		1794-1877 8812-8881		
The King's (Shropshire LI) (1882)	2	1800-1802 8882-8883		
86 (1759)	1	1781-1783 8884	1854-1907	1854-1907
Shropshire Volunteers (1793)		1793-1799 8885		
Leinster (1809)		1806-1877 8886-8947		
Royal County Down (1812)	2	1814-1815 8948		
2nd Bn Royal Irish Rifles (1881)	Dep			
87 (1759), Prince of Wales's Irish	1	1782-1877 8949-9016	1792-1907	1802-1907
(1793), Royal Irish Fusiliers (1827)				
Princess Victoria's (RIF) (1881)	2	1805-1818 9017-9022	(see also 89th)	
88 (1759)	1	1780 9023	1847-1917	1860-1917
Connaught Rangers (1881)		1794-1877 9023-9085		
	2	1804-1816 9086-9090		
see 94th	Dep			
89 (1759), Princess Victoria's	1	1780-1783 9091	1792-1907	1802-1907
(1866), 2nd Bn Princess Victoria's		1793-1877 9091-9164		
(Royal Irish Fusiliers) (1881)	2	1804-1816 9165-9169		
90 (1759)	1	1779-1783 9170	1807-1907	1809-1907
Perthshire Volunteers (1793)		1794-1877 9170-9237		
2nd Bn Cameronians	2	1794-1795 9238		
(Scottish Rifles) (1881)		1804-1816 9239-9243		
91 (1760)	1	1779-83,1793-5 9244	1797-1908	1801-1908
Argyllshire Highlanders (1794)		1798-1877 9245-9315		
Princess Louise's (Sutherland and	2	1804-1815 9316-9319		
Argyll Highlanders) (1881)	Dep		(see also 93rd)	
92 (1760)	1	1780,1793-5 9320	1816-1914	1816-1914
Gordon Highlanders (1794)		1798-1877 9321-9386		
2nd Bn Gordon Highlanders (1881)	2	1803-1814 9387-9392		
	Dep			
93 (1760), Highland (1799)	1	1780-3,1793-5 9393	1835-1902	1836-1891
2nd Bn Princess Louise's		1800-1877 9394-9456		
(Sutherland and Argyll	2	1813-1816 9457		
Highlanders) (1881)	Dep			
94 (1760), Scotch Brig. (1802-16)	1	1794-5,1798 9458	1826-1915	1843-1907
2nd Bn Connaught Rangers (1881)		1803-1877 9458-9514		
95 (1760)	1	1780-3,1793-6 9515	1839-1909	1839-1909
Rifle Brigade (1803-1816)		1800-1817 9516-9576		
Derbyshire (1825)	2	1805-1815 9577-9585		
2nd Bn Sherwood Foresters (Nott-	3	1809-1815 9586-9590		
inghamshire and Derbyshire) (1881)	Dep			

DESCRIPTION AND SUCCESSION BOOKS Years	WO25/ (uos)	SERVICE RETURNS No 1 WO25/	MMG's Cas. Index WO25/	INDEX TO CASUALTY RETURNS WO25/	CASUALTY RETURNS Years	WO25/	SOLDIERS' DOCUMENTS (Bn not specified) 1760-1854 WO97/	1855-1872 WO97/
1793-1831	498-503	1043	1322	2650	1809-1830	2073-2075	933- 941	1634-1636
1807-1824	504-505			2651	1809-1817	2076		
1855-1859	506 (1&2 Bn)							
1826-1866	WO67/20				1826-1830	2077		
1811-1833	507-510	1044	1323	2652	1809-1830	2078-2081	942- 949	1637-1639
				2653				
			1324		1825-1830	2082 (Dep)		
1806-1832	511-515	1045	1325	2654	1809-1830	2083-2085	950- 957	1640-1642
				2655				
					1814	2086		
					1826-1830	2087		
		1046	1326	2656	1807-1830	2088-2092	958- 966	1643-1645
					1856	2093		
		1047			1809-1817	2094		
1814-1816	516	1048	1327	2657	1809-1830	2095-2097	967- 977	1646-1649
1823-1830	517			2658				
1811-1828	518-519	1049			1809-1815	2098		
1828-1830	520				1825-1830	2099		
		1050	1328	2659	1809-1830	2100-2104	978- 985	1650-1652
				2660				
		1051			1810-1816	2105		
1804-1841	521-522	1052	1329	2661	1809-1830	2106-2109	986- 996	1653-1655
				2662				
1812-1831	523-524	1053			1810-1815	2110		
					1825-1830	2111 (Dep)		
1815-1831	525-526	1054	1330	2663	1809-1830	2112-2116	997-1005	1656-1657
				2664				
1814-1826	527	1055			1809-1815	2117		
1822-1831	528				1825-1830	2118		
1818-1843	529-532	1056	1331	2665	1809-1830	2119-2123	1006-1014	1658-1659
				2666				
		1057			1809-1814	2124		
					1825-1828	2125		
		1058	1332	2667	1809-1830	2126-2130	1015-1021	1660-1661
				2668				
					1814-1815	2131		
					1825-1830	2132		
1815-1830	533-535	1059	1333	2669	1809-1854	2133-2137	1022-1029	1662-1663
				2670	1825-1830	2138 (Dep)		
1816-1819	536	1060	1334	2671	1809-1831	2139-2142	1030-1037	1664-1666
			1335	2672				
		1061			1809-1817	2143		
		1062			1809-1816	2144		
					1825-1830	2145		

REGIMENTS OF INFANTRY Best known pre-1914 titles given with dates of original formation and renaming Foot	Bn	MUSTER BOOKS & PAY LISTS Years WO12/	REGIMENTAL REGISTERS Marriages Birth/Bapt Years Years
96 (1761) Queen's Own (1798-1818) 2nd Bn Manchester Regiment (1881)	1 2 Dep	1780, 1794-6 9591 1803-1877 9592-9650 1804-1814 9651-9654	1798-1818 1801-1818
97 (1761), Earl of Ulster's (1824) 2nd Bn Queen's Own (Royal West Kent) (1881)	1 Dep	1780-3, 1794-5 9655 1799-1877 9656-9724	1798-1908 1810-1908
98 (1761), Prince of Wales's (1876) 2nd Bn Prince of Wales's (North Staffordshire) (1881)	1 Dep	1794-8, 1804 9725 1805-1877 9726-9783	1878-1908 1879-1908
99 (1761), Lanarkshire (1824) Duke of Edinburgh's (1874), 2nd Bn Duke of Edinb.(Wiltshire) (1881)	1 Dep	1782-3, 1794-5 9784 1805-1877 9785-9846	1802-1908 1817-1908
100 (1761) Prince of Wales's Leinster (1858) (Royal Canadians) see 109th	1	1794-1797 9847 1805-1877 9848-9875	1812-1908 1812-1908
101 (1761) Royal Bengal Fusiliers (1861) Royal Munster Fusiliers (1881)	1 Dep	1794-1795 9876 *1806-1877 9877-9897 *(gap from 1818-1861)	1846-1908 1849-1908
102 (1761), New South Wales Corps (1798-1812), Royal Madras Fus. (1861), Royal Dublin Fus. (1881)	1	1793-1795 9898 1798-1818 9899-9907 1862-1877 9908-9922	1851-1906 1861-1906
103 (1761) Royal Bombay Fusiliers (1861) 2nd Bn Royal Dublin Fus. (1881)	1	1782-4, 1794-5 9923 1808-1818 9924-9928 1862-1877 9929-9944	1796-1914 1805-1914
104 (1761) Bengal Fusiliers (1861) 2nd Bn Royal Munster Fus. (1881)	1	1782-3, 1794-5 9945 1803-1817 9946-9950 1862-1877 9951-9966	1889-1908 1889-1908
105 (1761), 2nd Madras LI (1839/61) 2nd Bn King's Own YLI (1881)	1	1782-4, 1794-5 9967 1862-1877 9968-9984	1836-1913 1834-1913
106 (1761), 2nd Bombay LI (1826/61) 2nd Bn Durham LI (1881)	1	1794-1795 9985 1862-1877 9986- 10001	1844-1914 1858-1914
107 (1761), 3rd Bengal Inf(1854/62) 2nd Bn Royal Sussex (1881)	1	1794 10002 1862-1877 10003-10018	1829-1907 1836-1907
108 (1761), 3rd Madras Inf(1854/62) 2nd Bn R. Inniskilling Fus. (1881)	1	1795 10019 1862-1877 10020-10035	
109 (1761), Bombay Inf (1853/61) 2nd Bn P. of W.'s Leinster (1881) 110-135	1	1794 10036 1862-1877 10037-10052 1794-1795 10053	1854-1905 1854-1908

Rifle Brigade
  Rifle Corps (1800)
  95th (1803-1815)
  Rifle Brigade (1816)
  Prince Consort's Own (1862)
	1
	2
	3
	
	4
	Dep
		1816-1877 10054-10109
		1816-1877 10110-10167
		1816-1819 10168
		1855-1877 10169-10191
		1857-1877 10192-10211
		1873-1877 10212-10215
			Rifle Brigade
			has some
			Registers
			ca 1800-1914

DESCRIPTION AND SUCCESSION BOOKS Years	WO25/ (uos)	SERVICE RETURNS No 1 WO25/	MMG's Cas. Index WO25/	INDEX TO CASUALTY RETURNS WO25/	CASUALTY RETURNS Years	WO25/	SOLDIERS' DOCUMENTS (Bn not specified) 1760-1854 WO97/	1855-1872 WO97/
1779-1783	537	1063	1336	2673	1809-1831	2146-2148	1038-1043	1667-1668
1800-1818	538-539			2674	1849-1854	2149		
		1064			1809-1814	2150		
					1825-1830	2151		
1810-1865	540-546	1065	1337	2675	1810-1831	2152-2155	1044-1051	1669-1671
				2676				
1838-1855	547				1825-1830	2156		
1812-1818	548-549	1066	1338	2677	1809-1831	2157-2160	1052-1059	1672-1673
				2678	1842-1855	2161		
					1825-1830	2162		
1816-1833	550-552	1067	1339	2679	1810-1830	2163-2164	1060-1068	1674-1676
				2680				
					1825-1830	2165		
		1068	1340	2681	1810-1818	2166-2168	1069	1677
1810-1815	553-554	1069	1341	2682	1809-1817	2169	1069	1678-1679
1810-1815	555-556							
1814-1817	557	1070	1342	2683	1810-1817	2170	1069	1680
1815-1817	558		1343	2684	1809-1817	2171	1070	1681-1682
		1071	1344	2685	1810-1817	2172	1071	1683
							1072	1684
							1072	1685-1686
							1072	1687
							1072	1688
							1072	1689
							1072	
				2686	1817-1830	2173-2175	1073-1090	1690-1697
1800-1867	559-564			2687	1817-1830	2177-2179		
				2688	1816-1818	2181-2182		
1856-1865	565				1825-1830	2176 & 2180		

REGIMENTAL RECORDS

NOTES ON TABLES OF REGIMENTAL RECORDS IN APPENDIX 2 (pages 100-119)

1. Regimental titles and dates of formation. Titles of regiments have been taken from Brereton[4], Leslie[46] and the PRO List and Index Number LIII.[78] (The latter also includes a useful list of cavalry and infantry regiments which received numerical designations, as well as an alphabetical list of their colonels.) It is not possible, in the brief summary tables presented here, to give full details of the many changes in name of regiments, or of renumberings.

The earliest dates of formation of each regiment are quoted from the concordance of regiments given in the index to the first 40 volumes of the Journal of the Society for Army Historical Research (see page 80). Many regiments, from the 42nd Foot onwards, were disbanded at some time and so did not exist continuously from the earliest date of formation.

From 1881 many of the later-numbered foot regiments became second battalions of earlier named regiments, and so a cross-reference has been included under the first named. For instance, the 63rd Foot became the 1st battalion of the Manchester Regiment and "see 96th" indicates that the 96th Foot became its 2nd battalion.

2. Muster Books and Pay Lists (WO 12, 1760-1877). Piece numbers for particular years and further details can be found in List and Index Society Volume 210.[82]

3. Regimental Registers. These are held by the Registrar-General at St Catherine's House (see pages 21-22). This table includes only a summary of material given in the list on the open shelves there.

4. WO 25, Registers, Various. Piece numbers for particular years and further details can be found in PRO List and Index Number XXVIII[77] for Description and Succession Books, Service Returns Number 1 (24th June 1806), Muster Master General's Index of Casualties (1797-1817), Index to Casualty Returns (no dates or battalions specified) and Casualty Returns. (See also pages 27 to 28.) Description Books are from WO 25 unless otherwise stated (uos); Depot Description Books from WO 67 have been included in the table.

5. Soldiers' Documents (WO 97, 1760-1872). Piece numbers and further details can be found in List and Index Society Volume 201.[81] (See also pages 32 to 36.)

Bn = Battalion   MMG's Cas. Index =
Dep = Depot   Muster Master General's Index of Casualties
Mil = Militia   uos = unless otherwise stated

My Ancestor was in the British Army

INDEX

Army Lists   4-5
Army Records Centre   82-83
Army of Reserve   63-64
Artificers   45,59
Artillery   5,37,41-42,45-46,58
Australia   30,54,76-77,93
Auxiliary Forces   64-65,90-91

Baptisms   16,21-23,72-75
Barracks   21,68
Battles   24-25,90,98-99
Birthplace   38
Births   16,19-23,72-75
Burials   16,21-23,72-75

Canada   30,75,77-78,93
Cape Corps   49
Casualty Returns   26,28,43,100-120
Census Returns   19-21,68
Chaplains   60
Chaplains' Returns   21,23,74-75
Chelsea In-Pensioners   49
Chelsea Out-Pensioners
    Admission Books   46-48
    Admission Registers   31,46,48-49
    Deferred Pensions   50
    Discharge Documents   36,50
    Foreigners' Regiments   50
    Regimental Registers   46,48
    see also Soldiers' Documents
Civil Registration   17-18,76
Commander-in-Chief's Memoranda
    Papers   11-12
Commissariat Staff   12,61
Commissions, Purchase of   10
Commonwealth War Graves
    Commission   82-84,96
Corps - Various   59-61
Courts Martial   43,55-57,64,86-87

Deaths   16,18,21-23,72-75,84-85
Deceased Soldiers' Effects   69-70
Depot Musters   40-41
Description Books   45,100-120
Deserters   53-54,64,77,86-87

Diaries (War, WWI)   85
Discharges (1783-1810)   27

East India Company   49
Engineers   5,37,41-42,58
Enlistment, Place of   38

Federation of Family History
    Societies   68,97

Garrison Registers   74-75
Gibraltar   73-74,94
Greenwich Naval Hospital   49

Half Pay   10
Half Pay Ledgers and Lists   12-14
Hart's Papers   4,5,8
Hospital Corps   60,61

Imperial War Museum   85
Imperial Yeomanry   65
Indexes
    Card Indexes at PRO   16
    Chelsea Pensioners, 1806-1838,
    Beckett   66
    National Soldiers, 1792-1872,
    Beckett   67-68
    Other Ranks, 1861, Turner   67
    Regimental Location at Census
    Dates, 1841-1891, Holyer   21,68
    Various   97
    Waterloo, Saunders   68
India   30,80

Kilmainham   46,51-52
King's German Legion   12,49

London Gazette   79,86

Marriages   16,18,72-75
Married Establishment   42
Medals   24-27,70-71,85,92,98-99
Medal Office   70-71
Medical Officers   5
Medical Staff Corps   60-61
Military Labourers   61
Military Police   60-61
Military Train   60-61
Militia   12,15,37,42,45,49
                          62-64,65,90
Miners   45,59
Monthly Returns   20,24
Museums   69-70,92
Musketry (School)   60-61
Muster Books and Pay Lists   37-44
                               100-120
Muster Master General's Index
   of Casualties   26,28,100-120

National Army Museum   69-70
New Zealand   30,54,77-78,94
Nursing Corps (Queen Alexandra's
   Royal Army)   60
Nursing Service (Queen Alexandra's
   Imperial Military)   60

Ordnance see Artillery, Engineers
Ordnance Corps   60-61

Pay Lists   37-44
Pension Returns   26,29-30
Pensions, Widows'   14-15
Pensions to Wounded Officers   14-15
Photographs   86,96-97
Police Gazette   53
Prize Records   52
Public Record Office   - throughout
   the book   - references on 94-96
Purchase of Commissions   10

Red Cross, British   87
Red Cross, International   87
Regimental Number   39,43
Regimental Registers 21-22,100-120
Returns of Service (Officers)   5-9
Royal Wagon Train   60-61

Sandhurst   15
Sappers   45,59
Scutari Depot   37,42
Service Corps   60-61
Service Returns No 1 26-28,100-120
Service Returns No 3   26-27
Signals   60
Small Arms Corps   60
Society for Army Historical
   Research   80-81
Soldiers' Documents   26,31-36
                               100-120
St Catherine's House   21-23,84
Staff Corps (Royal)   61

Transport   60-61

USA   78-79,94

Veterinary Corps   60
Volunteers   12,64-65

Wagon Train   60-61
Waterloo Committee   68-69
Western Front Association   87
Wives   33,42-44
Woolwich   15

Yeomanry   12,49,64-65

Other Titles in the
My Ancestor series

My Ancestors came with the Conqueror - Those who did and some of those who probably did not, by A.J. Camp. Corrected reprint 1990, 84 pages.

My Ancestors were Manorial Tenants: how can I find out more about them? by P.B. Park. 1990, 49 pages.

My Ancestor was a Merchant Seaman: how can I find out more about him? by C.T. and M.J. Watts. Reprinted with addendum 1991, 84 pages.

My Ancestor was a Migrant (in England or Wales): how can I trace where he came from? by A.J. Camp. 1987, 44 pages.

My Ancestors were Baptists: how can I find out more about them? by G.R. Breed. Revised 1988, 51 pages

My Ancestors were Congregationalists - in England & Wales - with a list of registers, compiled by D.J.H. Clifford. 1992, 94 pages.

My Ancestor was Jewish: how can I find out more about him? Currently out of print - New edition available shortly.

My Ancestors were Methodists: how can I find out more about them? by W.M. Leary. 2nd edition, 1990, 74 pages.

My Ancestors were Quakers: how can I find out more about them? by E.H. Milligan & M.J. Thomas. 1983 (1990 reprint with minor alterations) 37 pages.

Other *My Ancestor* titles are in preparation.

These are available from the Society of Genealogists or from most good genealogical bookstalls. A current price list will be sent on receipt of a stamped self-addressed envelope.

My Ancestor was . . .

Is the title that you want missing from the list?

Are you knowledgeable on the subject?

- or do you know somebody who is?

The Society would like to hear
from potential new authors

Contact:

Series Editor: Mrs Jean Tooke
Publications Manager: Mrs Mary Gandy

Society of Genealogists,
14 Charterhouse Buildings,
Goswell Road,
London EC1M 7BA.

Phone: 071 251 8799